'79

THE SKA REVIVAL
DANCE CRAZE
ESSAYS FROM THE FRONTLINE
BY GARRY BUSHELL

First published in 2011 by Countdown Books Ltd
This edition © Red Planet Books 2019
Text © Garry Bushell 2011-2019

This edition published November 2019

Email: info@redplanetzone.com

Printed in the UK. by DG3

A catalogue record for this book is available from the British Library

ISBN: 978 1 9127 3313 2

REDPLANETMUSICBOOKS.COM

DANCE CRAZE

CONTENTS

INTRODUCTION

Hey, you, don't read that, read THIS! This is the heavy, heavy monster book, the nuttiest read around!

I t's also the only introduction you'll ever need to the boss sound of the Eighties: THE SPECIALS! MADNESS! THE BEAT! BAD MANNERS! THE SELECTER! and THE BODYSNATCHERS! With a saucy portion of Judge Dread thrown in for good measure...

It's hard to believe that 2-Tone took off 40 years ago (and even harder to credit that it's been 50 years since I bought my first copy of 'Liquidator'). Back in 1981 I wrote the original *Dance Craze* magazine that tied in with the film of the same name, with its companion fifteen track live album, celebrating 2-Tone's rags-to-riches glory. Our original idea in 2011, thirty years later, was simply to reproduce that magazine in an extended form. But when I reread it, I wasn't particularly happy with it. The mag had been aimed at young teenagers and was written accordingly. It was basic and flimsy; okay, but not good enough. I wanted to do the Ska Revival justice, and that meant rewriting pretty much everything and throwing in extra material and anecdotes from my note-books and diaries from the time about 2-Tone's invasion of the USA. I also added updates and a respectful tip of a pork pie hat to the Jamaican musicians who had pioneered Ska in the first place; because without Prince Buster, Laurel Aitken and the rest, 2-Tone would not and could not have happened.

I had lucked on to the story early, when, quite by chance I caught the first-ever gig that the Specials played as the Specials – just four hours after changing their name from the Coventry Automatics. To make the coincidence even sweeter, this happened in the summer of 1978 in my very first week of writing for *Sounds*, the late and truly great UK rock magazine which covered more rock, more punk and more reggae than any of its fancy-pants rivals. The Specials were supporting the Clash, who at the time were my favourite band in the world. I reproduce that positive review (published July 8, 1978) word-for-word later on in this book.

There were other attempts to merge punk and reggae around this time, principally from bands like those sound-of-the-suburbs pioneers The Members and the mighty Ruts, as well as the more successful but to my ears blander and more plastic New Wave reggae of The Police; but no-one did it as convincingly as The Specials.

After a delayed start, courtesy of the band's first manager Bernie Rhodes, The Specials grabbed 1979 by the throat and dragged it choking on to the dance floor. Within months they had gone from paying their dues at sweaty London dives like The Nashville and the Hope & Anchor to having two Top Ten singles under their belts and their own 2-Tone label, which opened the door for a new generation of top-quality Ska bands.

Among its many attributes, 2-Tone was responsible for putting character(s) back into the charts, real larger than life lunatics like:

Buster Bloodvessel, a moonstomping Michelin Man-shaped skinhead with boots, braces and a belly that quivered like a Quatermass mutation and who pumped out a massive 13-inch conger eel of a tongue – the kind of awesome organ that Soho's saddo mack-flashers could only dream of possessing.

Neville Staple, the Jamaican-born chancer with the roguish smile and boxer's physique, which ricocheted around every stage (and many a bed) in the land raucously roaring: 'HUSH NOW RUDE BOOIIZZZE!'

Chas Smash, a crazed Cockney kid in shades and a pork pie hat who danced like he was all elbows while fronting a human train of his Madness cohorts and hollering hoarse commands like "HEY YOU! Don't watch that, watch this!" as if you'd want to watch anything else.

Pauline Black, a hyper-active, heart-meltingly gorgeous Essex-bred Rude girl, bouncing around like an animated space hopper, running on pure adrenaline, and blessed with "the best voice that ever graced" the whole Ska explosion.

And in Pop Dream imagery, out there fronting the lot was Jerry Dammers, the 2-Tone ringmaster theatrically tipping his topper to Joe Public, unleashing a big toothless grin, and hammering at his Wurlitzer with the same insane nonchalance as Terry Jones on *Monty Python's Flying Circus*.

DANCE CRAZE

It was Dammers who made it all happen, with his single-minded pursuit of his dream; a dream that took old bastards like me back to the summer of 1969, when I was just fourteen, and the charts rang out with the joyous sounds of Desmond Dekker, Jimmy Cliff, Bob & Marcia, The Cats and the rest, and I blew my pocket money on them and more obscure singles by the Upsetters, King Stitt and Laurel Aitken which down our way could only be found at Muzik City, a shop barely bigger than a broom cupboard in Lewisham market (slogan: 'We got it from Lee at Muzik City'.)

1969 was the year of skinhead reggae when Britain's young working-class youngsters seemed to shave their heads en masse; a year of Ben Sherman and Brutus check shirts, monkey boots and Sta-Prest trousers, and for me at least a Trojan reggae disco above the Co-op Halls in Catford.

Dammers and co took that history and rebooted it for the next generation. And for a while they intensified it, turning vast sections of the charts monochrome.

Going to an early Specials gig was like walking into a world where all the other colours had been banned – like *Pathe News* had broken out all over. Black and white were the only colours fit to wear during the winter of '79. And the message was simple. On the surface it might have appeared to have all been purely physical – a case of, as the famous Madness slogan had it, 'Fuck Art, Let's Dance' – but the central message ran deeper. 2-Tone stood for unity; kids from all ethnic backgrounds living it up together as equals without all the middle-class social worker patronising.

As Gappa Henderson said succinctly back in the day: "2-Tone, black and white, that's the whole damn thing."

In a matter of months, 2-Tone rose from the small, sweaty clubs of Coventry and London to become a dance craze of feverish international proportions. It became the soundtrack to a million teenage lives, conquering the heights of the charts, brightening up many a dull *Top Of The Pops* Thursday along the way.

The scene rose up like a rocket, and for many of the bands, it seemed to fall away equally quickly. But the fuse they lit ignited scenes on every continent. And more recently all of them have returned playing sell-out tours, in the case of the Specials, and festivals and scooter rallies around the world; Madness, in particular, are still writing great music and playing impressive gaffs – Buckingham Palace!?! That's one hell of a step up from the Dublin Castle...

THE SKA REVIVAL

The 2-Tone flame has been picked up by a new generation of bands, such as Hackney's own Buster Shuffle and LA's incredible Interrupters who tour the UK in January 2020. Meanwhile, Britain's old-timers are still crafting quality material, like Neville Staple who is regularly gigging with his band, Judge Dread and Buster Bloodvessel's old buddy King Hammond and the divine Rhoda Dakar, when she isn't cooking in another woman's kitchen...

That's the problem with this kind of music you see. Once you get hooked, you end up Ska'ed for life...

Garry Bushell, 2019

PS. Some po-faced observers objected to the inclusion of Judge Dread in the first edition of this book on the rather tenuous grounds that he was "sexist". I can only assume that these joyless wretches have never listened to the early works of Max Romeo, Lee "Scratch" Perry, the Soulettes (featuring Rita Marley), Clancy Eccles, the Soul Sisters or Lloyd Chalmers of Bang Bang Lulu fame.

THE SPECIALS

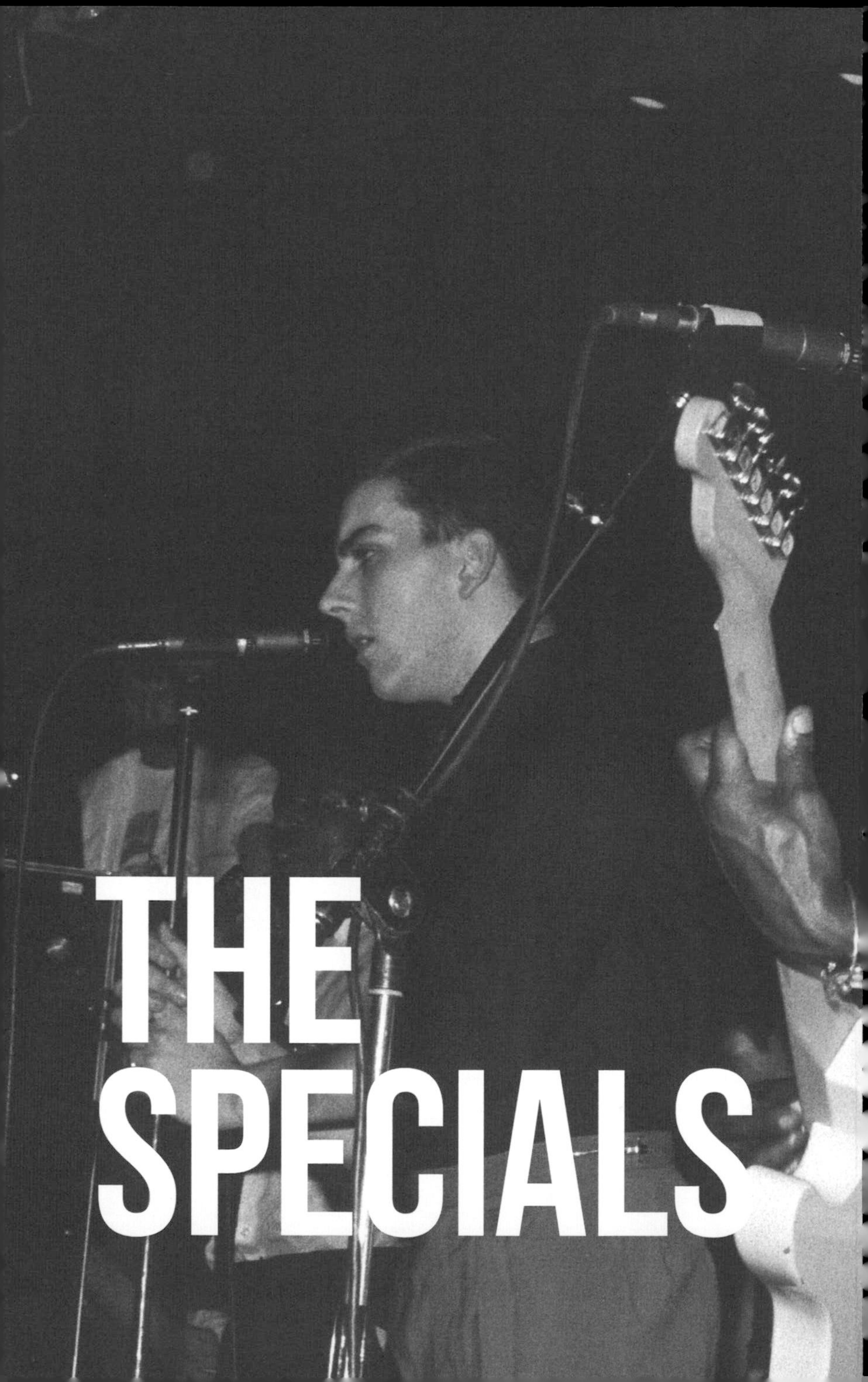

RUDE BOYS CAN'T FAIL

The Specials, New York, March 1980

WOW. New York, just like I pictured it. Skyscrapers n' everything... it's my first time in Manhattan as an adult, and I'm up early soaking up the grandeur of the great Babylon, those huge triumphant buildings standing proud against the heraldic blue of the sky. This is the greatest city in the world, for now at least: vibrant, can-do, aggressive and magnificent; a chest-beating, cock-waving monument to all-conquering capitalism; a "fuck you" middle finger salute to the world that can't quite disguise the fact that all of this fancy architecture is just a jog away from heart-breaking poverty. There's a bag-lady on the corner below, and we're a handful of blocks down the street from slums, muggers and junkie slime. In the midst of plenty...

"Oi Garry, you can't have a piss there!"

A rowdy Midlands accent rudely disrupts my meditations. I glance around to see a rogues' gallery of reprobates getting snapped for posterity by my infamous sidekick, Ross Halfin, the photographer known to *Sounds* readers as Gross Halfwit.

We're one floor up the concrete colossus that is the World Trade Centre and the paunchy out-of-town Yanks wombling past don't quite know how to take this disrespectful mob of uncouth Limeys who are cavorting and clowning around for a camera instead of paying homage to NYC's breathtaking self-confidence

The Specials, for it is they, are an odd-looking bunch: two quiet white guys in chunky all-American cardigans, a black bloke in a woollen hat, another black fella in a GI helmet and army green bomber jacket, a lairy-looking geezer in a tatty sheepskin, a 20-year-old in a white Harrington jacket and green tartan trousers with the staring eyes of a paralysed owl, and, strangest of all a yobbish chancer with no front teeth sporting DM boots, a soccer scarf and donkey jacket, who is much prone to making many strange ejaculations: "Gorblimey", he says. "On ya bike", "I'm fed up with all this homosexual phallic imagery", and so on. It's like a form of football-terrace Tourette's.

Above our heads, obscuring half a wall is a gigantic tapestry that looks like an Arab sheik's front room rug with a bad case of mumps. Donkey-jacket guy's chubby face breaks out in a huge cherubic grin. "'Ere, let's do one with this carpet," he hollers, and a respectable tourist behind me starts to tut loudly as the cheery hooligans form a painful looking human pyramid in order for him to swing on the mounted monstrosity.

"It's the closest you'll get to a good shag," remarks Halfin to a chorus of laughs and abuse. "2-Tone band in 'hard rugs' scandal," was the best I could come up with.

'Hey, stop your messing around/Better think of your future/Time you straighten right out/Creating problems in town...'

Outraged of Suburbia doesn't realise that he is tutting the driving force behind the hottest pop phenomenon of the moment, that this funny-looking fella with the missing front teeth is on the way to fulfilling a dream that he's been pursuing since his mid-teens.

JEREMY David Hounsell Dammers, known to a grateful world as Jerry, is not your run-of-the-mill pop star. Dammers is different, complicated. Some might say weird. A shy guy, he finds it hard to talk to people he doesn't know and on first meeting you could easily assume some village had lost its idiot. Unusually for someone in his position, Jerry isn't at all self-centred, and he nurtures an almost obsessive hatred of elitism, privilege and waste – the cornerstones of this marvellous little industry we call Pop with its legions of plastics, pretenders, parasites and budding Hitlers.

People who know him say his ambition isn't for himself but for his music, his dream.

Born in India, Jerry Dammers grew up mostly in the Midlands. His dad was a vicar, not particularly rich or poor, and he spent his teen years rebelling against his family background of restrictive Sunday righteousness. He'd drink too much, smash things up, run away from home – anything to get up his parents' hooters, to be different from them.

Most importantly, he got into music. The Who, The Kinks, the Small Faces, Otis Redding and Tamla Motown were his first loves, along with the joyous bliss of Trojan reggae. Even as young as 15, almost a decade ago, Dammers had the idea of merging rock and reggae together "although no-one in rock circles took reggae seriously back then." Over the years, four of which were spent in the pursuit of a fine art diploma, he slogged away in various pub and club bands trying to get them to play his songs with little success.

The Sex Pistols kicked open the door for a whole generation. And the idea, until then expressed only on home demo tapes made with the Selecter's Neol Davies, crystallised into something more than a dream. Exhibiting an almost frightening single-mindedness, Dammers built up the people around him who became the Specials by way of the Coventry Automatics. An odd bunch: two authentic rude boys (Neville and Lynval), two grammar school boys (Jerry and Horace), rocker (Roddy) and a punk (Terry).

THE SPECIALS made their debut at Aylesbury in July 1978 as a five piece. By pure chance, I was there doing my first ever review for *Sounds* and I wrote 'Whereas the Clash play punk songs and reggae songs, the Specials combine elements of the two. Yeah it sounds a phoney not to say disjointed formula but surprise, surprise, it worked.' Move over Nostradamus, you've just lost your crown...

Of course, I had no idea just how well it would work. The dream was still embryonic then and thanks to Bernie Rhodes that tour was the last we saw of the band till March '79 when a then-sane Dave McCullough rediscovered them and wrote the first-ever feature on the band. By then they were the real thing. Not just a working idea but a whole new music, a punky-reggae party – punk in feel and bite, Ska in the beat. The punk made danceable, the Ska intensified. The message: 2-Tone.

The history you know. They finally ditched Rhodes and their delicious DIY debut single 'Gangsters', on their own 2-Tone label, kissed him goodbye while cruising up the charts.

'Gangsters' was a re-working of Prince Buster's 1964 smash 'Al Capone', with lyrics taking their old manager to task: "Bernie Rhodes knows, don't argue!" The b-side was 'The Selecter' by the Selecter - Neol Davies and Ray Bradbury, with the trombone solo played, I'm told, by their local newsagent.

The Specials linked arms with PR man turned manager Rick Rogers and his Trigger crew and stood firm against a maelstrom of tempting record company offers until they got the deal they wanted from Chrysalis, a deal to make a dream come true with a surprising degree of autonomy to release what they wanted and sign who they wanted to their own label. Chrysalis cried all the way to the bank.

To date all of the 2-Tone releases have been Top Twenty hits, the Specials had three of them including the first 2-Tone number one with the Special

THE SKA REVIVAL

AKA Live ep in January. Their debut album was released in October 1979 and has shifted a cool quarter of a million' units' to date. The Specials have become more than a band; they're the ringleaders of a movement, the inspiration for a teenage fashion wave, and a brand-new dance.

JANUARY 1980 and the band hit America. Hard. Now it's the beginning of March and they've toured for five weeks solid giving the Police a good run for their money on a few dates but mostly headlining, sometimes playing an exhausting two gigs per night, and if you've seen the way they play you'll know what I mean by exhausting. Like at home, they've concentrated on small non-seated venues; the critics have wet themselves and the small part of America that's seen them has loved every bluebeat-backboned minute.

(One step) beyond the live shows, other developments are looking promising too. The album, repackaged here to include 'Gangsters', was released in January and has sold around 100,000 to date, reaching the 80 mark in the Billboard chart, itself virtually unheard of without a hit single (both Elvis Costello and the Police for example had hit singles before comparable album success).

Of course, the majority of US kids are still into disco or downers and wine at stadium concerts. But maybe the time is right psychologically for significant numbers of them to break away from the dominant dope culture that's held millions in its dozy grip for over a decade now.

After all, psychologically America is getting a good shake-up thanks to the Ayatollah – caricatures of the Iranian (counter) revolutionary nuisance, as twisted as any BM sticker of Asians, adorn New York. Maybe they'll be jolted out of their complacency. Either way, young America needs a music that doesn't sound tailor-made for lifts or funeral parlours.

"New Wave" is currently the hip craze in the States and the Clash in particular look set to clean up. The times, or at least the charts, could well be a-changing.

The usual 'informed rock commentators' didn't think the Specials would do as well as they have here. Which kind of made sense: who would have thoughts the Sherman Tanks would buy into their spirited mix of skinhead moonstomp and puritanical socialism? The big question now is: will the band carry on growing or run out of steam? The irresistible super-pop force of 2-Tone is meeting the immovable object of North American apathy head-on, and it's hard to tell what will happen.

Rude boy singer Neville Staple (born Neville Eugenton Staple according to his passport, in Manchester, Jamaica) is keener on

MR GEORGE

F & H Entertainments Limited, Lower Precinct Coventry

TONIGHT	TUESDAY
In Scene Two	In Scene Two
New Wave Reggae with	**DISCO PARTY NIGHT**
★ **THE AUTOMATICS** ★	
Plus Support Band.	*Plus Ladies Private Party Night*
20p admission with ticket or this advert before 10 p.m., 30p after	Free admission before 10.30 p.m.
	20p admission after 10.30 p.m.
Scene One available for private hire most nights of the week	Scene One available for private hire most nights of the week

commenting on the women here, and the madness of New York cabbies. "It's like, 'if you don't like the way I drive, stay off the pavement...'" he laughs.

But the band admits that financially the whole enterprise has lost around $50,000 to date – probably a conservative estimate – although that's got to be counterbalanced by album sales.

And the tour is obviously an investment for the future. Chrysalis Records clearly believe they could be on to millions which explains why the label's big brass executives are over from England for the last dates. The Specials ain't so sure.

"People are gonna ask us how the American tour went," says lanky bassist Sir Horace Gentleman (né Panter) "And I won't know, there doesn't seem to be any way of gauging it."

"It's been like gig-sleep-get up-travel-gig-sleep non-stop," owl-eyed Terry Hall affirms, "and most of the time playing two gigs a night – it's hard to make much sense of it. Personally, I don't think 2-Tone will be as popular over here as it is in England. Fashions don't tend to catch on in a big way over here, the country's too big."

Most of the band has enjoyed the States as an experience although for the black members especially the tour has opened their eyes to a few of the harsher realities behind the US liberal dream, as Lynval Golding (woollen hat and Ska guitar) testifies. Shaking his head, Jamaican-born Lynval tells me how he'd "walked into this shop in Chicago to buy a watch for my sister, me and Rex our roadie, and the guy says, 'Hey, you

can't come in here.' I said: 'What's the matter with you?' and as soon as
he heard our accents it was 'Can I help you, sir?' I told him to stick his
shop up his arse. Can you imagine how they treat American blacks in
that state?

"Another time I was in this bar in Boston wearing a green hat, and
this guy turned around with his mate and said: 'I like that hat – only
trouble is I don't like it on you'."

It's the same the whole world over – and that doesn't make it all
right.

As the gruelling tour progressed, tempers frayed and incidents like
that helped to keep the band together. That and the inevitable tour
anecdotes. Like veteran trombonist Rico sitting up all night hiding his
dope in his bible before going through Canadian Customs and then
getting busted for smuggling oranges (even though he'd brought them
over from the States days before).

In LA, they played eight shows in four days at the Whisky-A-Go-Go.
Roddy recalls sitting in the dressing room after the last gig dripping in
sweat to find a bunch of supercilious record company 'suits' waiting
for them. "I love that song of yours," said one, "'On My Radio'" (by
the Selecter!); while another asking if they could teach him to pogo.
"They wanted us to put our stage clothes back on and pose with them
for a photo," he recalls. "Jerry, who was really tired, just told them all to
'Fuck off!'"

Asked how he liked America, Dammers told the *LA Times* that he'd
had more fun on a school trip to Russia. On another occasion, Jerry was
called down to do a breakfast interview in New Orleans after a night on
the tiles. Always unpredictable he got up without warning, walked out
the hotel and straight into the swimming pool – fully clothed.

*'Call me immature, call me a poser/I'd love to spread manure in your bed of
roses/Don't wanna be rich, don't wanna be famous/I'd really hate to have the
same name as you...'*

When I first see him, he's in the lift of New York's Hotel Diplomat
and he looks like he's spent the last three hours listening to Public
Image on an empty stomach. Like drained, maaaannn. This and
tonight's gig do little to dispel my fears that maybe the tail end of the
tour wasn't the wisest of times to come over...

THE DIPLOMAT could well have inspired the band's 'Nite Klub', very
is-this-the-in-place-to-be, and what am I doing here? Mick Jagger, David
Bowie and Debbie Harry from Blondie all turn up tonight – cordoned
off from the swinish multitude of course, but even the punters seem

more hoighty-toighty than hoi polloi: the place seems to be crawling with trendies and posers who've willingly coughed up the rip-off five quid ticket price (thanks to big-time promoter Ron Delsener who gets 'Gangsters' dedicated all to himself) to be seen.

It wasn't exactly a bad performance, I've never seen the Specials play badly, but it was a bit lacklustre. They were obviously cream-crackered and there was no magic there, though this didn't stop the crowd going seriously barmy and demanding no less than three encores, the last one being an extended version of Rico's instrumental 'Man From Wareika'.

Even below par, the Specials, Debbie tells me later are "at least twice as energetic" as the average New York club band. Personally 'I wouldn't dance in a place like this; it's all a drag and the beer tastes just like piss...' crossed with anti-freeze.

The only thing that made the evening swing for me was meeting a party of Coventry rudies – Evo, Adam, Liam and Dennis; factory worker fans who've spent their holiday pennies coming over to see the Specials (and have had their hotel room paid for by the band as a return gesture). And even more surprising, errant Cockney Rejects fans Bovril Bob, Woolwich Mark and Paul Bradley who were over from London with the Jam; Weller and co were here too with Polydor A&R man and Charlton renegade Dennis Munday.

I went out on the piss with the chaps who were giving it the old 'Oily rag, spam' rhyming slang palaver to all-comers as they got increasingly Brahms and Listz. But you can drink anywhere, how often will a tosspot like me see Manhattan?

I discreetly slipped off to see the sights on me Todd. Big city, New York, bright lights, sure looks pretty, but believe me this time of night, in this weather, half-cut and on your Jack the Big Apple's more like a Granny Smith nipped by an early frost.

Back in the hotel room, though, I stare out the window at the Empire State and the Chrysler Building, and the sea of activity on the streets below, a world of corner delis, delivery men and doormen...as alien to the English visitor accustomed to UK licensing laws as the deep-fried knish the street vendors sell. That whole city that never sleeps thing is as true as the song tells you. New York, New York...so good they named it like a sitcom amnesiac; God's gift to grateful insomniacs.

NEXT DAY was the photo session and also the first time I'd really sat down for a proper chinwag with the band who are nowhere near as mean moody and difficult as their stage image might suggest. Terry in particular was an easy-going revelation.

THE SKA REVIVAL

I'd spoken to Jerry Dammers a few times before but only by telephone and that has always been easier because on the phone at his cluttered little flat in Coventry with his art school paintings on the wall and the postcard of Ken Dodd on the fireplace, he can be his real single-minded self, very concerned and finicky. In the flesh it's harder and he's obviously happier taking the piss out of the lovely Horace, picking up matchsticks and talking to them as if they were the lanky bassist.

No matter. Band philosophy has it that in no way is Jerry any sort of leader/spokesman. He'd probably string you up for suggesting it. They insist that the Specials are very much equal partners. Jerry's just the one who made it happen, the one who had the dream first of all, and believe me the dream is catching.

Back in England the dream has come in for some battering lately, mostly from Sounds resident reggae expert Eric Fuller whose comments have given the impression that 2-Tone represents the biggest carve-up since the Lord Mayor's Banquet. Fuller basically accused the band of ripping off Jamaican artists by half-inching their original songs.

Those initial broadsides seem to have unleashed a veritable orgy of anti-2-Tone feeling in the rock press. This week for example 2-Tone is variously "boring" (the scathing *Melody Maker*), "the rotting undergrowth of Ska" (*NME*), and "sickly exploitative Ska" (*Sounds*).

Strangely enough all the peddlers of trite, rehashed head music and elitist, completely ineffective 'radicalism', feel threatened by this morally impeccable dance music. Surely not because it's got through to ordinary kids, instead of sticking safely in University seminar rooms, and actually created a whole new ball game for hundreds of thousands of teenagers? Still the Grim Brigade draw up their battle lines and the Ska boys don't give a monkey's toss: 'If you don't like it you don't have to dance'.

These self-styled intellectuals are as out to lunch as a gluttonous fat cat with a no-limit expense account. In April last year one of their number described the Specials thus, 'dance music with a vengeance... the very finest pop songs...fresh and new and paradoxically familiar,' and made reference to the 'sheer integrity of Dammer's terribly effective lyrics.' What's changed? Success! The Specials crime has been to sign to a major company (while adamantly retaining their integrity), to become popular and to have Effectively Communicated. How damning! How pathetic...

LYNVAL Golding takes Eric Fuller's assertions more to heart. "What amazes me about the whole thing is that Jerry has just got to be about the fairest person on earth," he tells me. "I've known him for years and if there's even a half pence discrepancy with money he ain't happy, it all has to be shared.

"Jerry's got no interest in money, none at all. When we put in the musical quotations from classic Ska songs like 'Too Much Too Young' and the others, he tried to make sure the money would get to the right person. Cos in Jamaica everyone ripped off everyone but he'd keep on trying to find the real writer. As long as he's got his music, food and a place to eat Jerry's happy."

'I don't wanna be rich/Don't wanna be famous/I wouldn't wanna have the same name as you!'

Lynval goes on: "Now you take Rico," (Rico Rodriguez, who played trombone on the original of 'Rudy, A Message To You' and Prince Buster numbers like 'Barrister Pardon' and who along with flugelhorn player Dick Cluthell has accompanied the Specials on this tour and their last UK one). "We could be paying him a session fee but he gets the same as all of us and we're gonna bring his next album out on 2-Tone. Rico will tell you about Prince Buster and the way HE used to rip everyone off and how in the end no one would play with him. The reason Rico's stuck with us so long is that we've treated him fair and he's never been treated like that before."

Sadly, I never did get a chance to speak with Rico. There was a bit of trouble at Liberty Island, and then the band had to shoot off to Long Island for a sound check. I didn't get to the gig until hours later, but for once I arrived in style...

I am far too punk and bolshy to be star-struck but I will admit that as I was being driven in a huge black Lincoln stretch limo over the Brooklyn Bridge at sunset with Debbie Harry, the most beautiful woman in pop, sitting opposite me, her eyes so blue they made the Med seem murky, Chris Stein chopping out lines of cocaine and a magnum bottle of champagne on ice sitting in the corner, there was a fair bit of pinching myself going on, along with the recurring thought: wait till I tell 'em about this in the Swan in Charlton Village. (Sell out! – Ed.). This was the only time last weekend I really couldn't believe I was here...

Chris played us tapes of new New York rappers along with vintage Prince Buster songs and raved about the previous night's crowd. "The New York audience never gets like that except for the first twenty rows," he affirmed excitedly. But that night's gig at Speaks Club was even better. It wasn't supposed to be at Speaks, it was supposed to be at My Father's Place, but they couldn't cope with the ticket demand.

BACKSTAGE, the dressing room is over-run with rowdy rudies and band members, with old Rico with his dope watching through his slit-like eyes, and Dammers as ever collapsed in a corner snoring like a contented warthog. The band's laudably open attitude to having people in the dressing room stems largely from their experiences on the Clash tour in '78, when everyone was kicked out when Strummer and the boys were on stage and not allowed to scoff the food – the Specials had to hide in cupboards just to be able to get at something to eat.

I get Terry Hall, former clerical worker at a Coventry stamp and coin dealers, into a corner for a quick bunny about the future. The man the bungling *LA Times* called an 'energetic Jamaican' looks and sounds suspiciously English to these non-specialist eyes and he laughs much more than you'd have thought.

Seems the band are having one week off (apart from Xmas their first since September), then there's a one-off Paris gig, sort of a 2-Tone works outing, and then they're in the studio to lay down a few tracks from which a single will come although the boys are adamant that they won't be rushed.

Possible next number ones are Roddy Radiation's 'Rat Race' and Lynval and Neville Staple's autobiographical 'Rude Boys Out Of Jail' (Staple, the man behind the introduction of most of the 'musical quotations', in the Special's songs, did a sentence for burglary, affray and driving getaway cars before his current occupation as MC/vocalist and feels strongly about getting the 'prison is no fun' message across to potential villains in the crowd).

Possible future signings for 2-Tone are the Swinging Cats from Coventry featuring Jerry's girlfriend (Terry calls them "three brothers and an auntie") and from LA an all-girl sixties style New Wave pop band with punk roots called the Go-Gos who might be supporting the Specials here in the UK soon.

Then there's Rico's album, and Desmond Dekker has submitted a tape for consideration – 2-Tone's about ripping blacks off, can't you see?

Apparently, all the band have got new songs, Lynval wants to do his own album, drummer John Bradbury has a version of Rex Garvin And The Mighty Cravers' Sock It To 'Em JB' out some time (the only reason for the whispered new Specials' soul' direction it would appear).

There's also an idea for Neville and Madness's Chas Smash to do a one-off single with Neville as Judge Roughneck trying Chas for dancing too mechanically...And in the longer term there's dreams of launching their own recording studio, opening a club in Coventry, and generally building 2-Tone as the Tamla or Stax of our generation.

"We just want to make sure it stays a natural process," says Terry.

"And not get pushed in directions we don't want to go in. It may seem to have happened fast to you but really, it's the culmination of years of having nothing. We're not exactly rich now; the royalties won't really come through till later next year. But we wanna keep ploughing money back, which doesn't mean we're gonna go round saying we're gonna help Tom, Dick and Harry, but we will be an alternative for people who deserve the help and who want to use us."

MAYBE AN hour later Debbie Harry walks on stage like a vision and announces the band, and then Terry Hall adopts his Son of Rotten glowering stage persona to lead them on. At their first US gig he caustically announced: "This is it, my little petals, this is your last chance to dance before World War III" – so near the knuckle. Tonight, it's a sarky "This is our last show in America – you must have enjoyed every minute of us."

Hall comes across as a kind of depressed Dracula, with those big, burning eyes, deathly pale face and that alternatively hung-up and hang-dog expression. And he sings Dammers's sometimes funny, sometimes acidic words with a barbed bitterness.

Sometimes he dances on the spot, but mostly he's static, looking like the eye of a hurricane with his compatriots a whirling powerhouse behind him, especially the ultra-athletic Neville hurtling round the stage, balancing on speakers, be it sporting either a smart 2-Tone whistle or dressed up to the nines as Judge Roughneck or later stripped down to natty briefs as it gets TOO hot. (And he wants to show the girls what he's got...)

Lynval and Roddy, the gee-tar men do their lesser runs (Rod sometimes going through the complete set of Paul Simonon classic poses) while Horace moves gracefully, dancing with his bass held high. Then there's Brad at the back, a rock-solid anchor man (no nautical implications, JB), his drumming as aggressive and self-assured as the man himself.

AND FINALLY, there's Mister Jekyl and Hyde, Jerry Dammers. Put him behind his organ in front of an audience and all that off-stage uneasiness dissolves and we're left with an animated madman pounding away for dear life because his dream depends on it.

At one stage tonight he leaves his keyboards and just collapses on stage lying motionless till the near-naked Neville descends on him and perches on his back, and Dammers lifts his head to reveal a grin as wide as the Hudson River, the grin of a man totally content and gloriously optimistic.

FRIARS AT THE MAXWELL HALL AYLESBURY

THURS. JUNE 12

THE FRIARS AYLESBURY ELEVENTH BIRTHDAY PARTY 1969 ~ 1980

THE SPECIALS
THE BODYSNATCHERS

Tickets 300p available from usual outlets or at door (l.a.) Membership 25p

It wouldn't be enough to say they were good tonight. They were brilliant. Tomorrow they were going home and it was like they had to burn up every last drop of adrenalin left in them, amplified as the biggest dance beat around, transforming a rotten sweaty club in to the hottest place on earth with all the old favourites and the two new numbers, both bristling with a typical richness, morality and spiky dance attack, poured out in what even Eric Fuller would surely have deemed a well iry session.

Of course, it ended with a ridiculous number of encores, this time totally deserved. Lynval got so carried away he bounced right off the tiny stage, and right at the end Brad trashed his kit through pure passion. And there was me with a big dopy grin on my boat, thinking this is rock 'n' roll, these boys could be the real heirs to Chuck Berry and John Lee Hooker's thrones, the direct descendant of the glorious violent dance beat of primal R&B, carried across on the airwaves to Jamaica, reinterpreted as Ska, carried on to England, nurtured in bargain bins then finally mated with the white riot of Seventies English youth, the whole damn thing making for a passionate dance power that just cuts through all the phoniness, pretentions and corruptions of the contemporary music scene.

The next day I left behind the Lego buildings and lemming-like joggers of New York, secure in the knowledge that the band I'd been with are very special indeed.

POST SCRIPT. This account, a version of which was published originally in *Sounds* in 1980, was accurate but not entirely comprehensive. At the gig, demob crazy on our last night in the USA, Ross and I found ourselves chatted up by two no doubt short-sighted Brooklyn punkettes with accents broader than Central Park. We ended up inviting them back to the hotel. Debbie Harry was disgusted and I was shunted up front with the chauffeur in shame with both of the girls on my lap. This is when Claudia whispered in my ear: "My friend doesn't like your friend..."

Back in Manhattan, we lost Gross, found a dealer, drained the mini-bar and, let's just say that I enjoyed the kind of night that had so far eluded me after they called last orders at the Blackheath & Newbridge Working Men's Club. I've felt nostalgic about New York ever since...

Neville Staple had an unusual day too. A fan came up and gave the band a thank you bag of cocaine – about five grams worth. Nev shot off to the gent's to sample it, and as he was chatting to a fan by the cubicle, a fella with a mop of white hair breezed up and said, "Are you having a toot?" Nev recalled: "I looked up into the face of Andy Warhol...meeting one of the greatest living artists of the 20th Century in a bog in New York. What are the chances of that happening?"

POSTSCRIPT: I went to the USA with both the Specials and the Selecter at the beginning of the Eighties. Neither, the bands nor I had any idea how influential those few club dates would be. Over the following decade, a third wave of Ska, fuelled by 2-Tone, exploded in the US with bands such as the Mighty Mighty Bosstones (formed in 1983) from Boston, the Toasters (formed 1981) from New York City, and The Uptones (formed in 1981) from Berkley, California at the helm. The Uptones influenced Operation Ivy, who became Rancid, and an entire Orange County Ska scene which produced such exciting combos as the Aquabats and Reel Big Fish. The Bosstones helped popularise the new ska-punk sound which merged the two musical forms, playing Ska at a punk pace. Ska-Core later blended Ska with hardcore punk. But bands like the Toasters went for a more 2-Tone influenced traditional Ska style. Singer Robert' Bucket' Hingley launched the hugely important Moon Ska Records label, whose latest incarnation, Moon Ska World continues to release great Ska acts such as and the Dub City Rockers, The Big and the brilliant but almost obsessively argumentative Rhoda Dakar...

In 2011, the Specials were back together (without Jerry, who said they sacked him) playing to packed houses for whopping fees. Jerry was still performing with his Spatial AKA Orchestra. (see Epilogue)

****

AFTER-Thought: 2-Tone went up like a rocket and then fragmented into a hundred pieces. Why? "2-Tone fell apart because Jerry really controlled it all," Suggsy told me in 1984. "It was one person's ideas controlling 32 people and when you think about it why should all those bands have carried on succumbing to his dream? I think the whole idea of 2-Tone was much stronger than the actual music. It became a musical fad which is why I think it got eaten up and burnt out so fast. The ideas meant much more…"

While it was united 2-Tone spelt marvellous times live, and undoubtedly the best came with the 'Taking It To The People' 2-Tone tour in November '79 which saw the near-perfect package of the Specials, Madness and the Selecter selling out Top Ranks, Tiffanys and polytechnics with the same ease as their skanking singles were sailing up the chart. Mostly it was laugh-a-second stuff. I caught the show at Tiffany's in Edinburgh and can still grin at the memory of all three bands finishing the night off with a mass recital of the ol' Skinhead Moonstomp.

There is little doubt that the 2-Tone bands helped to change opinions and stem a rising tide of racism in the UK. 2-Tone didn't spawn a Hitler Youth following. On the contrary, it boosted the ranks of anti-racists and non-racist skinheads, reaching out to black, mixed race and Asian kids like no UK youth cult had done before.

In February 1980 the second UK 2-Tone tour repeated the sell-out success of the first, this one featuring The Selecter as the headline act, the Bodysnatchers as the show openers and as main support the promising

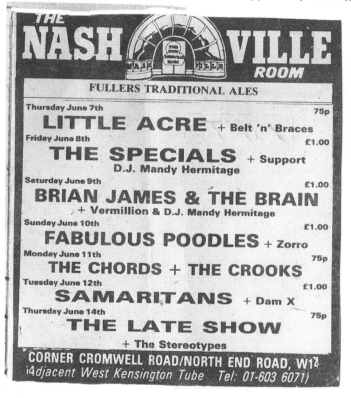

pop act Holly & The Italians – a last minute replacement for The Beat. Trouble was the exciting eyeties weren't Ska and the whole tour was disgraced by audience birdbrains abusing them for that heinous non-conformity. Fighting frequently broke out during their set, so the Italians retreated to be replaced by The Swinging Cats who later signed to 2-Tone.

THE SKA REVIVAL

Jerry Dammers found this narrow-mindedness abhorrent. He had no intention of sitting pretty in a musical cul-de-sac. Instead he guided the Specials along more experimental tracks, perfecting a mix of styles, including muzak, trad MOR and even Latin American rhythms to produce the 'lounge music' of the Specials second LP *More Specials*, which spawned the haunting hit singles 'Stereotype' and the addictive 'Do Nothing'. Internal dissent about direction coupled to the strain of making the 2-Tone movie *Dance Craze* led to the Specials line-up splitting in '81, but not until after the atmospheric chart-topping 'Ghost Town' had provided the perfect soundtrack for that summer's riots.

Out of the split, Hall, Staples and Golding emerged as the Fun Boy Three scoring a string of deadpan hits and launching Bananarama on the road to stardom in their own right, before splitting themselves in '83 leaving Hall to form the under-achieving Colourfield.

For his part Dammers recruited a new line-up, including vocalist Rhoda Dakar and much later temperamental new boy Stan Campbell, called the band the Special AKA again and spent over two years and half a million pounds making a follow-up LP. Called In The Studio, this passionate pop cocktail, drawing on a mixture of reggae, funk, jazz, afro, gospel and Latin rhythms suffused with haunting melodies, was a vibrant testimony to Dammers' abilities even though it was top-heavy with already released singles like the ethereal, anti-Zionist song 'War Crimes' and the well-meaning but arguably wrong-headed 'Racist Friend'. Best moment on it, and indeed the single of '83, was the clenched-fist protest of 'Nelson Mandela' – Jerry's last-ever Top Ten hit.

Commercially Madness fared much better releasing the healthiest, and most diverse string of hit singles since the Beatles. They even broke into the US market, scoring a Top 10 hit in '83 with 'Our House', something the Specials and the Selecter had both failed to do despite their club success in the USA's 'armpit' cities of LA and New York, although the watered down white reggae of the Police went platinum there. The only threat to their robust run came at Christmas '83 when Mike Barson, the uncrowned band leader and keyboardist co-writer of all their best tunes, quit. Madness quit Stiff the following summer and had hits for a few more years on their own Zarjazz label. Suggsy also lent his production talents to Liverpool terrace popsters The Farm.

Poor old Selecter never seemed able to harness their live energy into a lasting studio career. Their first three singles, 'On My Radio', 'Missing Words' and 'Three Minute Hero' were fair to sensational but thereafter their releases seemed to lack the sparkle that had made their live shows so special. They just sounded too earnest. Increasingly pissed off, the band split from 2-Tone and decided to change direction. The likeable Desmond Brown quit while he was ahead while Charley Anderson was mysteriously sacked (going on to form not very special band the People). They were replaced by a couple of white guys from the Pharaohs. The new band slowed down the former frantic Selecter pace, softened up, aimed to be more soulful…and still flopped. They split altogether in 1981, with Pauline Black attempting a solo recording career before coming into her own on the TV where she graduated from presenting kids show *Hold Tight* to serious/dull Channel 4 chat show *Black On Black*.

Meantime the mighty meaty Bad Manners had a string of sporadic hits on Magnet until 1983. Finally realising that the label was holding them back, they quit in '84 but never bounced back into the charts.

For their part the Bodysnatchers never really cut it on vinyl, evolving into the Belle Stars in 1981 who went top three two years later with 'Sign Of The Times' and then faded away; while the Beat notched up a string of seven hits before Ranking Roger and Dave Wakeling quit in 1983 to form General Public who never got higher than Number 60 in the charts.

Back in '80 Dammers steered the 2-Tone label away from straight ska and consequently away from hits. The biggest tragedy was the failure of Rico's Sea Cruise to chart – his *Jungle Music* LP was rightly heralded as a possible new direction for reggae but sagged disappointingly on the sales front as well. Flops from the Swinging Cats, the Apollinaires and the Higsons were both more predictable and more deserved. However laudable Jerry Dammers' attempts to widen the range and appeal of the 2-Tone label, it clearly wasn't what the people wanted. As the bands went their separate ways and no new 2-Tonic talent came to fill the clubs and pubs they'd left behind, so the magic and the sense of unity fell away and with them the Rude Boy cult. At street-level the skins found solace in the new Oi! Movement, while the best 2-Tone bands deservedly went on to become part of the pop establishment. For myself however, the image stamped on my brain from this era isn't one of any of the bands on *Top Of The Pops*, but rather one from after the Selecter had finished their 'James Bond' encore at their Birmingham Top Rank gig. As the band trotted off stage, there was a stage invasion and a white Rudy grabbed the mike and started chanting 'Rude Boys'. Spontaneously, he reached out to a black Rudy. They put their arms round each other and gave the crowd thumbs up signs. That simple image probably says more about the 2-Tone dream than any words ever written.

MADNESS

DANCE CRAZE

BLUE BEAT & PORK PIES BRITAIN IN THE GRIP OF MADNESS

Edinburgh, November 12, 1979

'MADNESS, MADNESS, THEY CALL IT MADNESS... I"M ABOUT TO EXPLAIN, THAT SOMEONE IS LOSE THEIR BRAIN, HEY MADNESS, MADNESS, I CALL IT GLADNESS...' ('MADNESS')

THE SKA REVIVAL

SOD THIS for a game of soldiers. It's 8.45pm on a Monday evening, and it is officially thirty degrees below Margaret Thatcher. It's cold, rudies; so cold that even happening band Madness are in danger of being downgraded from HOT to lukewarm. So cold that photographer Virginia Turbet's merkin is likely to migrate south for the Winter at any minute. Brrr. I may be stuffed on Stiff's freebie food and booze, but if they think for one micro-second I'm standing here turning blue...

Of course, any sensible soul would be at home with their feet up watching Porridge, and yet the doors of Edinburgh Tiffany's club are chock-a-block with chilly billy-bunters in their tartan scarves, thermal kilts and frosted sporrans. Like me, the kids (© Jimmy Pursey) are bursting guts, toes, bladders and patience to get in out of the sub-arctic temperature and we are all getting nowhere fast. I look around in vain for a friendly St Bernard bearing brandy.

Scotland's capital city has, it would seem, been earmarked by some chinless government weasel as a testing ground in some fiendish mass freezing experiment, and quite frankly brass monkeys and mouldy taters don't come into it, pal. This frozen crowd make Adam Adamant in his block of ice look like John Bindon on the sun-kissed beaches of Mustique.

Ahead of Virginia and I, Stiff's token Scottish PR Andy Murray attempts to clear a path by handing out free Rachel Sweet singles to the Old Bill and almost gets nicked for his pains. Time for a few porky pies: "Scuse me mate I'm the bassist," Virginia claims illogically but loudly. It works! The crowd make like the Red Sea and Moses, leaving us free to swagger past the surly cops and straight through the doors, so we can thaw out and mark time at the jolly old bar until...it's show time!

This very first 2-Tone tour has lured more hardy explorers out into the life-threatening cold than the call of the North Pole. And quite rightly. This is the greatest show on earth (for now at least), and young Scots Ska fans are here to bop until they drop to the non-stop, no-flop, mega-pop sounds of our current chart favourites...all for just £1.75 a head. What a bargain! Come on, folks, roll up, roll up, we're robbing ourselves here, and if we get six months you won't wanna be doing three of 'em. Going once, going twice, going, uh-uh, three times...

The Specials, Selecter and Madness are the name of tonight's game, the sound of 1979 (with just a sprinkling of notable exceptions). 2-Tone's souped-up Ska sparkle is merrily moonstomping its way up the charts and selling out the nation's polytechnics, Top Ranks and Tiffanys with this current, mammoth 'taking it to the people' tour.

But my brief for today's roaming in the gloaming exclusively concerns Madness and a feature of the Big One variety. Tuesday morning's BRMB chart shows their first Stiff single 'One Step Beyond' skyrocketing up 29 places for a brief respite on the back of those two little ducks, all the 2's, 22, before possibly catapulting them all the way into the Top Ten. Their debut single surprised everybody by going Top 20 from nowhere. Suddenly every A&R man in London descended on their gigs like thirsty tramps on a cider farm. Chrysalis and Virgin wanted them badly, but it was Stiff Records who got the band's inky 'x's on the contract – and then only because the label's big cheese Dave Robinson hired them to play at his wedding! (Dave later recalled: "They even got Elvis Costello to dance which was unheard of. They literary dragged him onto the floor...")

And now Madness are back in the Top Thirty for the second time this year, the second time in ten weeks in fact. Not bad going for a self-confessed "bunch of absolute knobs." Yet four months ago few people outside of their mums had even heard of them...

Backtrack: I was stuck on a five hour train journey from Glasgow to London in the summer of '79 with no buffet and with only the company of ex-Pistol Paul Cook to keep me from crawling up a wall, and unless my memory deceives me he spent a good half of the ride rabbiting on about this band called Madness who came from Camden Town and who were apparently a good laugh and well worth the effort of seeing.

As it happened a couple of days later I saw them advertised as playing the Moonlight Club in West Hampstead and thought I might as well check them out. It was a decision I've never regretted. It was just then that the hipper kids were waking up to the Specials, and obviously the whole Ska revival was new to most ears.

I'll admit that the first time I saw Madness the band didn't impress me as much as either the Specials or The Selecter had done. The Nutty Boys had some good numbers sure, but with their lyrics lost in the mix, they did seem, in retrospect, maybe just a couple of steps beyond pub rock. Good pub rock, maybe, but pub rock all the same.

Similarly, the debut 2-Tone single 'The Prince' was decent enough but not as awesome as either its Special predecessor or Selecter successor, or indeed their b-side cover of Prince Buster's golden oldie 'Madness', from which the band took their name. This was the song that hinted of the greatness to come. Fact is it wasn't till the release of their debut album at the end of last month that cynics were thoroughly convinced about the band. One Step Beyond finally put the North London combo in a proper perspective, illustrating firmly their joint parentage – the glorious sixties Ska of the aforementioned

Prince Buster and the joyous Cockney vignettes of Mr Ian Robin Dury, whose abracadabra I'm particularly partial to.

The slower numbers in the set suddenly began to register. Like for example bassist Mark Bedford's 'Mummy's Boy' with its jokey, jerky foundation for excellent Lolita reminiscent lines such as: 'Once went out with a London girl/Dirty weekend in a hotel/Broke it off when she got shirty/She was twelve/He was 30...' (Kind of Dury meets John Peel, that one). Even better was vocalist Suggsy and guitarist Chrissy Boy's 'In The Middle Of The Night' which in typical New Boots style sketches out the outlandish character of an underwear thief, or knickers-nicker, called George: George is described as a nice guy, a happy 63-year-old news agent with a permanent smile on his face, a whistle on his lips, and an unhealthy secret burning a hole in his conscience. For at night, the jolly shop-keeper has a tendency to trespass through back gardens helping himself to armful of ladies' undercrackers that had been foolishly left on the line.

The old fool's wretched double life only comes into the open when, one day, he isn't around to open his paper shop. Suggs has to go further down the road to buy his "Currant Bun" (Sun), only to discover George's picture on the front page. Geo has gone away to stay with mates "he got the paper early and saw his own face." Oh for the days when mere knicker-nicking was a front page offence...

Saxophonist Lee Thompson's borstal broaching tale 'Land of Hope & Glory' has a similar Duryesque flavour, leading our office cynic to the conclusion that, "Ian Dury wouldn't record another *New Boots and Panties* so Stiff got someone who would."

The album is much more than that however, for me capturing the essence of teenage working-class London: a bluebeat base forged from too many Saturday nights beneath plastic palm trees mixed with breezy love songs and Cockney character sketches; the whole lot embellished by the band's perpetual striving after their own Nutty Sound (cue the usual 'sounds of summer fairgrounds' allusion).

Now you can properly appreciate their potential. They're altogether less intense, more, how else can you say it, nutty than their sometimes bleak Coventry colleagues. Madness are tapping in to rich veins of Cockney culture and English humour. If they keep building on that, who knows how big they could be.

Madness haven't quite perfected the Nutty Sound yet musically, though they're breathing down its neck with the cheery Wurlitzer bounce of their budding, Yakety Sax Looney Tunes style instrumentals. And visually Chas Smash sums up the whole concept with his nifty nutty dance and multiple shouts of: "HEY YOU! DON'T WATCH THAT WATCH THIS!", "CHIPMUNKS ARE GO!", "ONE STEP BEYOND!", "THAT HEAVY, HEAVY MONSTER SOUND, THE NUTTIEST SOUND AROUND" et al.

Chas's close-cropped kid brother Brendan Smyth, a rascal who's working on tour as product salesman and patience tester, is also a keen supplier of nutty phrases, such as "I've had a touch," (he's certainly touched), "Over and out," "Kamikaze!" and "On the case!" (If I were tour manager, I'd be on his case like a hotel porter chasing tips).

Brendan is joined on the band's travelling periphery by manager John 'Tin-Tin' Hasler, roadies Chalky and Toks (drummer Woody: "If Toks pushes you backwards, you know that Chalky will be kneeling behind you") and usually an away team of devoted fans including Totts and Whets, not to mention Lindsay, Wandsworth Harry (who apparently still owes Chalky £12 quid) and the fabled Prince Nutty. (At this point I'd like to mention my Uncle Bern too, because he's never had a name check in Sounds either).

THE BAND proper are Lee 'Kix' Thompson (saxes, some vocals, falling off chairs, walking socks, crew cut shades and 'burns); Chris 'Chrissy Boy' Foreman (guitar, Barry Sheene lookalike, family man); Mike 'Monsieur Barso' Barson (ivory-tickling, shades, infant moustache); Daniel 'Woody Woods' Woodgate (drums, vegetarian, Mo-Dette girlfriend); Mark 'Bedders' Bedford (bass, smiles, uh, bass); Chas Smash (shouts and t'ings), and Graham 'Suggsy' McPherson (vocals, vodkas, Leveller exposes).

The band hails from the Camden Town area of London, not that far a hike from the Cockney heartland of St Mary-le-Bow's in Cheapside. Their influences emerge quickly. One of their earliest musical activities was following Ian Dury's earlier band Kilburn & The High Road in the wee years of this decade, Lee especially becoming great mates with the Grand Old Raspberry and is 'umper, Fred 'Spider' Rowe, and mightily bewitched by the Kilburns' saxophonist Davey Payne. The bluebeat bite came via Lee, Suggsy, Chrissy and Chas's private childhood record collections. For Suggsy and Chas, Ska and Trojan reggae were an important part of being skinheads which they were for years before the 1978 skin explosion ("When Sham come along I grew me hair," says Suggsy, cuttingly but not entirely truthfully).

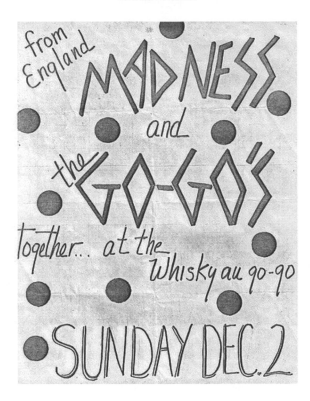

from England MADNESS and the GO-GO'S together... at the Whisky au go-go SUNDAY DEC. 2

Chas developed his unusual dance routine while pissing about to 'Liquidator' by the Harry J. Allstars (never complete to my mind without the "Skin'eads are back!" crowd chants as punctuation).

What we're really talking about is a group of teenagers, some mates, some mates of mates getting into music and eventually putting their own band together. Mike Barson could play the piano and he taught Chrissy the basic guitar chords. In 1976 they formed their first real band, the Invaders (AKA the North London Invaders) with Lee on sax, Chas attempting to play bass, manager John Hasler then on drums and various bods including Hasler trying out as vocalist.

Their musical approach was similar then, albeit far less successful, and they stabilised their line-up last year, changing the moniker at the Music Machine in Camden this January for the much more concise and definitive Madness. Progressing through pubs like the Dublin Castle and the Grope & Wanker (Hope & Anchor – Impatient Translator) they were naturally intrigued by early media reports about the Specials. Extended feelers on both sides resulted in valuable support dates and contacts at a time when music paper hacks were starting to get wind of the whole new scene.

Reviews in *NME* and *Sounds* followed, chased hard by a feature in *Sounds* in July, their debut one-off single on 2-Tone in August, Stiff signing in September (just three weeks after playing at Dave Robinson's wedding reception), the release of their debut album in October and the start of this titanic tour. That's one hell of a ride.

SEPTEMBER, October, No wonder I'm here, battling with barmaids who've never heard of light 'n' lagers and hiding my pad and pen so I can forget about taking notes and just soak up the show. And no I'm not going to get into the whole who-outplayed-whom argument at this stage; suffice to say none of these bands are third class tickets, and Madness in particular have tightened up (reggae pun, be still my aching sides) almost beyond belief and are currently a more than fair investment for your hard-earned LSD.

Their set, for those who like to know these things, is: Tarzan's Nuts, Mistakes, Believe Me, the sublime My Girl, Swan Lake/ Razorblade Alley, Land Of Hope & Glory, In The Middle Of The Night, Bed & Breakfast Man, One Step Beyond, Rockin' In Ab, Nightboat To Cairo, Madness. Encore: The Prince ("Guess who this one's dedicated to...")

Live, the band is a real visual treat – as lively as you like, funny and easy to love. During the tightened-up Tchaikovsky reworking of Swan Lake, Suggs and Chas (the self-styled Coco Brothers) bump bonces – real nut crackers, see - and go through some pretend aggro moves while moving completely in time with the beat. On 'Night Boat To Cairo' (which comes with fog horns and sax as raspy as a smoker's cough) the two twerps remove their pork-pie titfers and put on fezzes. By Tommy and Cooper! They're natural clowns, these boys, the point where Ska meets slapstick and whacks it in the mooey with a big fat custard pie.

Chas Smash wasn't even in Madness to begin with. He was a fan who, according to Danny Baker, "raised stage invasion into a fine art" and in the process became 2-Tone's first authentic star. Watching Madness for the first time, Chas (real name Cathal Smyth, Carl to his friends) was always the one you remembered the most. Most of tonight's audience are seeing all these bands for the first time live, and the beams on their faces say it all. This was worth risking hypothermia for. The most moving moment of the entire night however is the final encore, after the Specials' own sparkling performance, which featured all three bands and several fans dancing through that old Symarip classic, 'Skinhead Moonstomp.' (Chrissy Boy tried to entice me up for vocals but, sad to say, I lost me Aristotle, thus preserving the ear-drums of many an unsuspecting Edinburger.)

Puritanical viragos will be pleased to learn that there was a notable absence of both booze and carnal conquests back at the hotel after the show. Most people just hit the hay. Given the number of excited women-folk at the gig, that really was madness.

Brekkers the next morning is a hectic, not to mention chaotic affair, what with Selecter Desmond Brown hollering for bloodclaat bacon sarnies and Neville from the Specials dishing out random insults a la "Rasclaat", along with hangover-aggravating shouts of "MONKEYMAN!" My, the staff look pleased. Before too long, the carnage spills over into the hotel foyer which rapidly turns in to Casey's Court as well, with poor old Andy Murray flying around like a blue-arsed fly, tugging lumps out of his barnet, trying to organise his troops for photos with Virginia Turbulent and then, ta ra, the serious interview...

'FUCK ART LET'S DANCE' is the Madness slogan. The band themselves don't put much store on the old jaw-jaw either and are keen to leave out any highfalutin' sociological ramifications to what they do, and what 2-Tone is. However, unfortunately, any Madness feature would be incomplete without some discussion of their sometimes heavy skinhead following, including a solid lump of neo-Nazi British Movement numbskulls who recently went completely out of order bottling Orchestral Manoeuvres In The Dark off stage at the Electric Ballroom. In return Madness fans got indiscriminately attacked by misguided and heavily tooled-up anti-fascists at Hatfield Poly earlier on this tour (see footnote)...

The band's sincere anti-racist stance has not subsequently been helped by an article in the *NME* which dumbly misinterprets Chas Smash's comments about neo-Nazis in their audience to make it look as if Madness has no problem playing to extremist rightwing thugs...

"Now personally I hate all this BM business," says Labour voter Suggsy. "But a lot of the kids get taken in by it. When I was 13 all the kids used to go down Brick Lane in the East End, where that lot sold their papers, and it's easy to get pulled along by all of that; which is precisely why I don't turn round and say 'Kill 'em all.' They're just

NUTTY NEW SINGLE FROM
MADNESS
'THE PRINCE'
OUT NOW ON
2 TONE

ordinary kids being like their mates, and the BM thing gives them a sense of identity. That's all. It doesn't mean a lot to most of them outside of that. The way I see it, if they're all dancing to black music that means more than shouting at 'em or slicing 'up up. Personally I'm more worried about violence at our gigs..."

Chas agrees, adding "If they fuck around at our gigs we don't wanna know. They're out"

Suggsy goes on: "These kids fight all the time; it's what they do for fun. So we say just don't do it at the gigs...obviously it'd be far better if they didn't do it at all..."

Chas recalls three kids who the band had banned because of the trouble that they had caused trouble at Madness gigs. He says: "The other day the three of them came up and asked if it was alright if they came back and promised to behave. Because they do care, y'know. Underneath the front, they care."

"Yeah," agrees Suggsy. "Don't forget that at the Dingwalls gig, it was the skins who went around stopping all the trouble."

"One thing you can never do is generalise about skinheads," says Woody sagely. "And when the audience get dancing there's nothing else on their minds except enjoying themselves. But we get all kinds at our gigs, not just skins."

Suggsy sums up the band's aims succinctly. "Entertainment," he says firmly. "The nearest thing you can say is that all we want to do is have a good time, get better at what we're doing, people enjoy it, make some money and be successful. We're not trying to read anything deep into it."

I MANAGED to extract plans out of 'em: they'll leave the 2-Tone tour after the next two Scottish gigs (they'll be replaced by Dexy's Midnight Runners). Then there are three London home crowd shows at the Electric Ballroom followed by their first foray into the USA – a nine day One Step Beyond Tour of small clubs and kharzies. ("We wanted to get there before the Specials, and we did," Suggsy told the music press later). Then it's back to rehearse new numbers – they've got four in the pipeline, before they head off on a headlining UK tour of their own. More dates, in Europe and hopefully the USA, will follow before they go into studios in March, with a view hopefully to releasing their second album in April. Busy boys, eh?

They have some nice things about Stiff Records, and they ask me to convey another cryptic message to a certain 'Mr Bentley' ("We warned him but we still beat him to it – though he's probably still in with a bit of a chance... he'd better watch Spider though, he reckons he's gonna come with us. Says it's more of a laugh.") And then the lovable lunatics are spirited away on the coach for Rufles in Aberdeen.

I remember watching them nutty train their way through the hotel's revolving doors, sinking back on the bar stool and thinking how the perfect metaphor for Madness would be a couple of comprehensive kids bunking off school one May Day, dodging the train fare down to Margate, and spending the whole day pissing about in the famous Dreamland funfair, pulling birds, pigging down chips and getting legless on cheap lager...That probably just about sums the nutty spirit up.

THE US gigs Madness played were small but well received, and they did go back to North America in February and early March but this heavy workload took its toll leading to the other dark side of the band's story. The lads all took holidays, but a couple of them took drugs as well.

Skinny drummer Woody wasted away to just seven and a half stone. Each of Madness found their own way of coping with the pressure of their mammoth "Ska Trek" touring marathon: booze and fags, or dope, cocaine or speed. "It's so easy to get hold of drugs in the music business," Woody confessed. "And at the start they help, but then you find you have to take more and more of them to get by or to get the same buzz. You end up being depressed when you take them because you know you shouldn't be taking them, and depressed if you don't take them because you kid yourself that you need them. You become addicted, psychologically at least... and then it rubs off on the band because you make mistakes on stage. We ended up making so many fluffs we thought that we would blow everything. It frightened us."

Suggsy was convinced for a long time that Madness would crack the States. They had one hit in 1983, with 'Our House' – which was more than their 2-Tone label mates ever managed – but that was it. Bedders later admitted: "We did loads of small clubs but during our set everyone there seemed to be playing pool. It was lots of hard work for very few sales." While Woody explained: "The only thing they know about reggae in America is Bob Marley. They don't know the difference between Ska and dub. All black music to them is either soul or disco."

Madness did notch up a superb run of UK hit singles, however, from 1979's The Prince to Waiting For The Ghost Train in 1986: twenty-three of them, including fifteen Top Tens. In the Eighties they spent 214 weeks in the UK singles charts; and chalked up four platinum albums, four golds and two silvers. As well as multiple appearances on *Top Of The Pops*, the Nutty Boys were invited to perform on the supposedly grown-up rock show the *Old Grey Whistle Test*, where the sound was cack, and the band later dismissed the crew forcefully as "a joke." "All the guys who work on Whistle Test are pissed out of their brains all of the time," an aggrieved Mike Barson claimed libellously in *Melody Maker*, adding "The woman who's supposed to run the teleprompt fell off her chair when we were there... she just sparked out." Far better was the band's appearance on the legendary kids' TV show *Tiswas*, even though Chas Smash did manage to terrify the poor old Phantom Flan Flinger off camera.

Yeah Madness were the big winners, and grinners of the 2-Tone revolution. In the end love and laughs trumps preaching and bleak political realism every time.

FOOTNOTE (from my book, Hoolies): October 27 1979. The 2-Tone tour, featuring Madness, The Specials and The Selecter, rolled in to Hatfield Polytechnic. Disaster ensued. The audience, a mix of students, straights, mods and skinheads, had been good-natured and upbeat. But, when the Selecter started their set, a tooled-up mob calling themselves the Hatfield Anti-Nazi League burst into the venue through a plate-glass fire-exit door and started to indiscriminately attack and stab blameless skinheads in the audience. It was the worst violence ever seen at a UK Ska gig.

The anti-fascists – in fact, members of the far-Left Socialist Workers' Party – claimed that there were National Front members present. Madness fan Nikki Clark was just one of the many innocent bystanders who remember it differently: "There had been no trouble; everyone was in a good mood. Then this lot just broke in and started cutting any bloke who had short hair. It was awful."

Another eyewitness was mod ace face Grant Fleming. "There were about thirty of them,' he recalls. 'And they were really tooled up. They smashed in at the side of the hall level with the front half of the audience, who were mostly skins, and started properly slicing people up. It was nasty. The doors flew open, the windows smashed in – it was a proper attack. It was also dark and the band was playing so it took everyone completely by surprise. People were panicking. They couldn't work out what was going on, or why it was happening.

"They were after skinheads, specifically NF skinheads, but how they could tell what someone's politics were by their clothes escapes me. Obviously they couldn't and people were getting stabbed and hurt just for being skins.

"Before the gig, me and about five mates had gone into a pub near the station which turned out to be their pub. They saw me in my red Harrington with the Union Jack and flew through the bar at us. Luckily, one of the local kids knew us and said, "They're all right, they're mod boys." We drank our pints pretty sharpish.

"A few of them were older than us. They were an odd-looking group – they weren't mods or punks. They weren't anything. But they were game. We weren't expecting the attack on the gig; no one was. It was the worst violence I had ever seen at a gig, until the Battle of Birmingham with the Cockney Rejects, which was worse but in a different way. There were a lot of things being thrown at us in Birmingham. Here it was a tooled-up gang attacking individuals, and because of the savagery and the severity of the attack people kept away from them; they didn't want to know. It was a nasty night, vicious and pretty horrible."

Ten people were hospitalised, there were eleven arrests, and £1,000 worth of damage was caused. Madness's tour manager, a likable character called Kelloggs, was sacked by Stiff Records for having taken the night off, although it's difficult to know what he could have done to stop the premeditated carnage that unfolded.

The SWP later expelled the men behind the attack, denouncing them as 'squadists'. They went on to form Red Action, a militant pro-Irish Republican far-left grouping.

The far-Right had every reason to hate 2-Tone – it was the antidote to their poisonous message of racial hatred. At a Bad Manners gig at the Electric Ballroom in Camden the following year, a notorious neo-Nazi (a BM member later heavily involved with the violent neo-Nazi group Combat 18) leapt on stage and tried to stab Buster Bloodvessel; mercifully, Louis 'Alphonso' Cook smashed him off stage with his guitar. But at Hatfield the far-Left had been completely in the wrong; their brutal approach was wildly misjudged and utterly counterproductive, having the effect of attracting real neo-Nazis to future gigs.

There were more political problems at the band's Electric Ballroom that followed. Chas Smash described it as "the worst gig ever...it was like a bloody political rally. The Young National Front were passing out leaflets at the Lyceum the week before saying 'We want a good turnout at this gig'. And then all the mods and glory boys were going round saying the same thing to each other, you know, 'Should be a good bundle, lads'. What could we do?"

At the gig, Madness had a good local R&B band called Red Beans & Rice as support. Red Beans had two black members and when they went on stage the racist element in the crowd started to sieg-heil at them. Suggsy, Chas Smash and his brother Brendan who had all been watching from the wings jumped into the sea of skinheads and confronted them. Suggs reportedly put a couple of them in hospital with a microphone stand.

Very few of the trouble-makers even understood what sieg-heiling stood for. As Mike Barson said at the time: "All that bloody right-wing stuff is just fashion. Half the kids down the squats at Kings Cross where I used to live are looking for a bit of excitement, they're just bored. One week they're in the NF, the next it's the BM. If you try and have an intelligent conversation about it, they've no idea what they're talking about."

Ugly scenes like this briefly put an unfair stain on the band who had set out to be the antidote to politics. Lee Thompson was adamant that their mission was to keep everything "fun and humorous, almost as a rebellion against the punk thing. We've always wanted to keep music away from politics. Music should be fun, and above all, loving."

By the following March, the political controversy and the warring halfwits it attracted, had died away enough for Bedders to joke to the music press about Madness record royalties going direct to the National Front ("That was an actual rumour we heard, no kidding!"). The violence and the negative press led to the band having to face record company executives in the WEA boardroom (they were signed to Sire in the US, who were owned by WEA). Chrissy Boy had to assure them: "If we had wanted to go into politics we'd have formed a debating society, not a band."

The Madness boys were no strangers to gig aggro though. The band first encountered problems when they were the North London Invaders and they played the Acklam Hall in West London. Like many later bands would do, they made the mistake of taking their mates. The Ladbroke Grove Skins reacted badly to the sudden appearance of a bunch of North London skins on their patch, and turned up to the gig forty-handed.

Suggsy recalls: "Someone burst into our dressing room with an iron bar." Chas Smash, who was a fan not a band member at the time, adds: "I was on speed and we had a fight in the toilets."

Chrissy Boy: "We were pushing our vans to get them started and get away and one of the vans backfired. They thought we had a gun. Someone shouted 'Oi! They've got a shooter!' Funny now, but at the time..."

Chas: "The band drove off and the police escorted the rest of us through the LGSs who wanted to do us."

Suggsy: "Going to someone else's area with a load of your mates was taken as a threat. People would prepare for you to come and give you a welcoming committee."

Trouble dogged the early Madness gigs too. Suggsy describes them as "rough times, we had to break up fights in the audience and jump offstage. There were stage invasions, stages collapsing, local rivalries – you had the Bridlington mods versus the Bridlington skins. Every fucking gig was just chaos."

It's little wonder then that as the band grew bigger and more popular they started playing matinee shows so their younger fans could see them in stress-free environments. Stress-free for them, and for Madness themselves.

The band went on from strength to strength until Christmas 1983 when Mike Barson, the uncrowned band leader and keyboardist co-writer of all their best tunes, quit. Madness left Stiff Records the following summer and had hits for a few more years on their own

Zarjazz label (a subsidiary of Virgin Records). Suggsy also lent his production talents to Liverpool terrace popsters The Farm.

In 1985, they released their first Barson-free album, *Mad Not Mad*, with Barso's keyboard parts supplied by Steve Nieve from Elvis Costello's Attractions. Later Suggsy would accurately dismiss this album as "a polished turd." The first single, 'Yesterday's Men', peaked at Number 18 here, the next 'Uncle Sam' only made it to 21, the first Madness 45 not to go Top 20. The subsequent single, a cover of Scritti Politti's 'Sweetest Girl', crashed and burned at 35...

They were in the process of writing the next album when they finally announced that they were splitting for good in September 1986, citing the old chestnut "musical differences." Barso came back for the farewell single, '(Waiting For) The Ghost Train' which at least saw them back in the Top 20, so they could bow out on a high. For what happened next, see the Epilogue.

THE
SELECTER

RUDIES UBER DALLAS

Texas, May 1980

letting it go to their heads, and that big yellow sun that looks like it's just come unstuck from a packet of Cornflakes. Yup, it's pow'ful hot in Texas, boy. Pow'ful confusing too...

It was my idea to drag the Selecter along to Southfork Ranch in Plano, so that we could all pose ironically of course under the famous sign familiar to all viewers of TV's Dallas, and maybe snatch a glimpse of knee-high nympho Lucy Ewing (the soap's poison dwarf) in her bikini. Or at least catch Miss Ellie hanging out her smalls. Except now we're here, Desmond Brown doesn't look too impressed. "Where's all the oil wells, mister?" the organ-grinder moans. "I thought this was Texas!"

Bob Marley lookalike Charley Anderson swings his skinny, dipstick frame up on to the ranch fence, looking like an over-sized stick insect in Compton Amanor's huge, bug-eyed shades. "One day boy, all this will be yours" he drawls, his shock of red dread-locks shaking in merriment.

Move over Larry Hagman, there's a new boss in town. JR is now officially Jah Rasta, for just a dog-gone minute at least.

Arthur 'Gappa' Henderson laughs and grabs a handful of bush which he sucks on like a yokel's straw in a perfect country bumpkin impression. "Yippie", "yee-haw" and "howdy y'all" we yelp and holler to unimpressed passers-by. Dang, this is fun. "We ought to do a Ska version of the Dallas theme for our next single," grins Neol Davies. With 'Rawhide' on the b-side, I suggest.

But then we notice that the Selecter's paunchy tour driver Romain Reynolds isn't laughing.

"In this state, the people who own the ranch have the right to shoot you dead for trespassing like y'all just did," he grumbles. And just in case we think he's laying it on thick, Romain points out the bullet holes in the side windows of the bus where furious locals had let fly at the last band he'd been transporting around the Deep South. You don't get that with Dolly Parton, who Romain normally drives for, a fact he mentions just once or 97 times.

If that's not enough to dampen our spirits a flat-bed truck motors in from Hogge Road carrying four burly geezers who look, aptly enough, about as happy as a herd of prime pigs in a pork pie factory. The temperature is high, somewhere in the Nineties, yet the looks they're giving us are nippier than topless night in an Eskimo bar. One of them is clearly caressing a baseball bat. He doesn't appear to have a ball.

Romain wanders over and a heated conversation ensued. He comes back grim-faced and tells us to get on the bus and keep quiet. It's only later that we find out how frequently the word 'nigger' had figured in their exchange. Don't you love it when a Klan comes together?

THERE'S racialism the world over of course, but in our limited experience of Texas the bigotry seems different here. In-bred, institutionalised. The norm. "Appalling," Selecter singer Pauline Black observes simply.

So where will that leave a bunch of mixed-race Brit bluebeaters with a message of 2-Tone tolerance and implied socialism? Strung up in front of burning crosses was one particularly vivid vision in my jet-lagged mind. Another involved multiple Mafia bullet shots from a grassy knoll.

"It's different for the Selecter," Romain explains. "Because they're a band and because they're British. But there are still a lot of places I wouldn't take them." Without changing his expression at all, he adds, "Why, only last month in my home town they shot a black man dead for being down town after dark." So a little bit more of a challenge than playing Manhattan or LA, then...

It's true to say that Pauline nearly died on this tour. But that wasn't down to any good ole boys and their Louisville Sluggers. It was more a case of her not reading the instructions on the water bed in her motel room. "I was pretty exhausted after our second US show in Portland, Oregon," the Queen of Ska recalls. "And I just collapsed onto my bed as soon as we got back from the gig. A couple of hours later, I woke up feeling like hypothermia had set in! You're not supposed to use the bed without heating it up first. They had a little typed notice telling you this but I hadn't seen it. I dread to think what would have happened if I hadn't woke me up. They'd have probably found my corpse in a block of ice. Seriously, it took two hours for my teeth to stop chattering."

Charley suffered for his art too. When the Selecter played Los Angeles, they stayed at the famous Tropicana on Santa Monica Boulevard, where the bassist managed to put his back out in the shower while entertaining a couple of fans, who just happened to be female, and gorgeous, and naked. Talk about Too Much Pressure.

Charley was in so much pain the band had to scrap two shows. The bill that followed the subsequent visit from Jack Nicholson's chiropractor is believed to have hurt even more. Naturally at the time, the press were fed the bullshit PR line that he'd pulled a muscle leaping about on stage.

The Selecter hit Canada first in mid April, and have been doggedly slogging their way around the USA ever since to the same kind of small but solidly fervent adulation that had greeted earlier 2-Tonic forays by the Specials and Madness, selling out respectable 1,000-capacity venues to the hip tip of the vast US audience iceberg.

Last October's 'On My Radio' single has been selling steadily on import, Stateside. *Too Much Pressure*, their debut album was released here at the beginning of March, impacting on all three of the major US charts. It was still rising slowly as I caught up with them. The influential trade mag *Billboard* had made the album its hit pick one week, while the *LA Times* ran a glowing front page review of the band. The UK *Sun* has been over. Even those hippy horrors at *Rolling Stone* are covering them.

A-List stars are turning out for them too. Bubbly Bette Midler burst in back-stage at LA raving about the band – David Bowie had apparently slipped her a seven-inch (writes Benny Hill) in New York last December.

Singer Marsha Hunt came by the Tropicana to interview the band – Pauline reveals that Desmond's opening line to her was "I've always wanted to fuck you." The smooth-talking bastard! (Well he is the organist...). While strolling bone Mick Jagger and Jerry Hall turned up at their Hurrah's show. And danced too...

Not a bad draw for Coventry's most motley crew.

Alas, there was no stellar turn-out at the Dallas Bijou club. No JR, Bobby, or lip-quivering Sue Ellen. Neol Davis, the main brain behind the whole Selecter enterprise, and a man described by Ms Black as "Fonzie without the muscles" fills us in on the evening's schedules. It seems that Pauline & co will be performing between the resident heavy metal band and a Wet T-Shirt competition. Photographer Ross Halfin's face lights up. Ms Black noticeably winces.

THE SKA REVIVAL

We arrive to find an audience of caricature cowpokes straight from central casting. The geezers sport a veritable sea of ten gallon hats, checked or embroidered shirts, denim, rodeo belt buckles and snake-skin boots. The womenfolk are similarly attired in tight shirts, tight shirts and cowboy boots. Most of them are on the dance floor grooving to FM radio schlock. Like Donny and Marie, they're a little bit country, a little bit rock 'n' roll; but not at all Ska. Only two locals have made any kind of effort to get into the contemporary mood. One cheeky chap has gone for a 1977 stereotype punk look, including the bondage strides, while his mate boasts an ill-fitting pork pie hat. And that's it. For the rest, it could be a day out at the rodeo. When the disco stops, the women clear the floor.

The humorous potential of the occasion isn't lost on Pauline who sets a perhaps unnecessarily sarcastic tone as soon as the band takes the stage. "Are you gonna sit down all night?" she asks, wide-eyed. "Ain't any of you Southern gentlemen got any manners? Stand up! Thank you." So not such a sweet black angel after all...

The audience is understandably bemused. They've never had a Ska band here before. The Selecter are boldly skanking where no be-crombied Brit has ever skanked before. But in fairness, in the South, we may as well be Martians. These are truly alien rhythms here. Ska was just a flash of the pan in the US, just a couple of minor hits at the turn of the last decade. Most of this lot probably think Burning Spear was a 1950s b-movie Western. And now this sassy school ma'am type, this well-spoken Romford-raised British beauty is having a pop at them for the benefit of her pals' amusement. It doesn't seem entirely wise, and even the presence of massive Cockney minder Steve English doesn't put me at ease.

And yet, it works. One by one, the punters are poked, prodded and persuaded to take part of that irresistible Selecter Big Bounce, that meaty chugging beat that's welded tighter than Rod Smallwood's wallet to moving melodies and handsome hooks. The resulting colourful musical tapestry belies the band's puritanical appearance...

Pauline has always been the main draw for me, a hyper-active and heart-meltingly gorgeous Rude Girl bobbing and bopping, prancing and dancing, running on pure adrenaline with a voice, like her big bouncing breasts, that is an instrument of wonder. What's that? I shouldn't mention the breasts? You try avoiding them, pal. A lesser man would be inserting ten-gallon brassiere gags into this piece with a crowbar. (Even Bette Midler was intrigued enough in LA to ask whether her strenuous activities hurt her boobs. But nay, she says. Apparently, Playtex helps, but I'm too scared of her to ask.)

Pauline is as sexy as she is feisty and it'd be hypocritical not to acknowledge that most of the men in the audience would love a shot at being her Three Minute Hero.

The guy you notice most on stage is Gappa Hendricks. He's big, black and looks meaner than an Attica State Prison inmate. All through the set, Gaps stares, and snarls, and smoulders like any minute he's going to explode and tear someone's head clean off.

I saw them first at the Lyceum in London last year when they'd absolutely stolen the show from the Mod headliners, demonstrating that although Secret Affair's Ian Page was right and the time was most definitely right for a new dance, it wasn't quite the one he was expecting.

In Sheffield a month later, I saw the full set – and Gappa at his most aggressive. As the band prepared to play 'Too Much Pressure' – the b-side of 'On My Radio' – you could almost see the steam coming out of his ears. Gappa let loose a stream of indecipherable Jamaican patois. "Too much bloodclaat pressure," he growled as the band lay into the meaty, beaty, big and bouncy body of the song. It was then that he decided to live up to his stage image of the kind of guy who'd use sulphuric acid for splash-on deodorant by suddenly erupting and lunging at Charley. And with Charley knocked scatty, Gaps turned and aimed himself at Desmond before hurtling back to knock smack bang into guitar star Neol.

Charley stripped off his jacket and with his immaculate six-year-old dreadlock mane flapping in unconcealed (mock) rage he steamed into his assailant reducing the stage to a sprawling mass of flying fists while, strangely oblivious to the aggro, drummer Aitch (Charles H Banbridge), keeps pounding the beat. The music never stopped.

This scene is re-enacted in Dallas. Sadly, Charley's back problems mean he can't be as spirited as usual, but this is the sort of action the cowboy crowd appreciates. They whoop, they holler, they climb on chairs to stare at the unexpected aggro, a heaving sea of limbs and heads and moans and groans building to a climax where rhythm guitarist Compton is triumphantly hauled upside down and shaken silly.

It's only then, as the band immediately gets back to business, that the punters realise that we've all been party to well-acted, pre-planned frolics.

'Visually exciting' is a term readily applicable to all the 2-Tone bands and the Selecter are no exception. Live it's a case of light the blue touch paper and stand well clear. Nina Myskow described their performance style as being 'stolen from a frog on pep pills.'

Like the Specials, the band hailed largely from Coventry proving that the West Midlands city had more to offer than Chrysler, the Sky Blues and memories of Lady Godivá's mammaries. The original Selecter recording, on the b-side of the Specials' debut single, had all been guitarist Neol's brainchild. But by 1979 they'd become a fully fledged gigging entity. Neol recruited the all-black reggae outfit Hard Top 22 and wooed them away from the rootsy Rasta sound that was their forte.

The Selecter share origins and ideals with the Specials, but they're not the same animal. Whereas Dammers and co mix ska and reggae with punk rock, the Selecter sound is more, as Pauline puts it "rock, reggae and soul." They're not reviving the past, they're revitalising it – using that Jamaican base to forge something new, vibrant and cross-cultural.

Neol Davies, the quiet man behind it all, shuns the limelight and modestly refuses to take the credit for Selecter's success, but it was Neol who wrote all of band's great original songs.

His influences are more home-grown than you might imagine: Duane Eddy and Hank Marvin were his early guitar heroes, and The Beatles and The Who provided the sound track for his teens. Neol lived on the same Coventry street as the Specials' original drummer Silverton Hutchinson, and it was Silverton who suggested getting him in to play rock lead guitar over reggae music with Chapter 5, their band at the time. Charley

Anderson recalls: "Neol rehearsed with us in the cellar a few times and performed two gigs with Chapter 5. The first one was nearly a disaster. Neol's guitar was so loud that we nearly got canned off the stage! People weren't used to it in reggae clubs." Their second gig was on the back of a truck, presumably for a quick get-away.

Recording the instrumental track 'Kingston Affair' gave Neol the idea of

forming a band of his own – it was him who persuaded John Bradbury of The Specials to buy a drum kit. That band was called The Transposed Men – he took the name from a sixties comic book cover. It featured Desmond Brown on the Hammond organ, as well as Kevin Harrison (later of Urge) on guitar and Steve Wynn (later of The Swinging Cats) on bass. Neol's 'On My Radio' was the high-point of their set.

For Pauline, then known as Pauline Vickers, seeing the Foundations play at her Essex school was the first big changing point in her life. And being chatted up by them – the first black men she had ever spoken to – that made her re-think pretty much everything about herself. Adopted by a white family, she was the only non-white kid in her entire neighbourhood. She left home to find herself, discovering the joys of sex and alcohol along the way.

Pauline was studying biochemistry at Coventry University when she watched a female folk singer strumming her way through an acoustic set at the backroom folk nights in her local pub, the Old Dyer Arms pub in Spon End. Inspired, she bought herself a guitar and learnt to play it. But it wasn't until she saw Mick Jagger live that Pauline understood how to do it properly – and realised that the only way for her to enjoy performing was to go out and grab an audience by the throat. She ended up getting kicked out of the folk club for an over-enthusiastic, booze-fuelled interpretation of 'Honky-Tonk Women'.

Jazz singer Billie Holiday and Joan Armatrading were who Pauline listened to at home, though, especially winding down after her long shifts at Walsgrave Hospital where she worked as a radiologist.

A local musician, a black radical called Lawton Brown realised her amazing vocal talent. They started writing songs together and he took her to see Hard Top 22.

By chance, Pauline used the same rehearsal studio as the fledging Selecter. It was Lynval Golding from the Specials who spotted her talent and put Neol and Pauline together. Neol recalls, "It was obvious she was the singer to make the songs work. It call came alive very quickly when the seven of us were together."

She gratefully accepted his offer to complete the band. Last year, she turned pro, and doesn't seem to miss her old life one bit. "At the hospital, I was cleaning up balls of pus, puke and worse," she explains. "You name it, I cleaned it up. Particularly the posteriors after barium meals and enemas." So literally a shit job...

Charley Anderson, the other crowd pleaser, grew up in Montego Bay. His Mum brought him and his five siblings to the Motherland when he was eleven years old – his Dad had pissed off to the States. Seeing Jimi

Hendrix on Ready, Steady, Go was all the catalyst he needed to get into music. Charley faced rejection from local kids, white and black – he was too black-skinned for the white kids, too light-skinned for the black ones.

Desmond has known him since Charley was fifteen. "Me, Charley and Lynval from the Specials used to play together in a soul band, and then we had a reggae band but we were never in to the heavy reggae, the dub side, more the uptempo stuff, the fun stuff," he says. Desmond cites his organ influences as Booker T, Jimmy Reed and perhaps more surprisingly Dave Greenfield from the Stranglers.

I first met him at Charley's humble abode in Hillfields, Coventry, after seeing the band's Sheffield gig. I'd been soaking up the atmosphere – and sifting through Chas's record collection of vintage Toots and Prince Buster singles – when Desmond decided I was a mite on the shy side and that strangulation was the best remedy. Thanks pal. Kids, do not try this at home.

The Selecter really came into their own live where most of the band work themselves into a frenzy strongly resembling a hornets' nest ten seconds after it'd been struck with a house brick, while pumping out their over-powering rhythms. Only Neol is the exception. He's happy to do little on stage, preferring to impersonate a paralysed version of the 2-Tone symbol man Walt Jabsco.

'On My Radio', a dynamic take of fickle passion and fossilised programming, was their first UK hit and 2-Tone's third...

BACK in the Bijou, the band is wearing down what's left of the audience's resistance. Pauline never leaves them alone for a moment, while Desmond deserts his Hammond to hare through them, attracting almost as many amazed stares as the "ruck 'n' roll" panto section. Incredibly the Texan punters reward them with not one, not two but three encores – a splendid 'Last Train To Skaville', a Gappa dominated 'James Bond – De Killar', and 'My Sweet Collie' (Millie's 'My Boy Lollipop' subverted into a toast to the old Bob Hope) followed by a final, fraternal rendition of 'Madness'.

And that was it, the band cleared the stage, the FM disco kicked back in and then we got the Wet T-Shirt contest – various buxom blondes vying to out-do each other on the big boob/erect nipples front for a panting cluster of excitable Yanks and the despicable Halfin. I haven't seen so many wobbling chests since that Buster Bloodvessel lookalike convention. THERE'S a lot to like about Texans. They are fiercely independent, tough, resilient, hard-working can-do people; they've got no time for anything as poncy as the welfare state and collectivism that the British have grown up with. But that I'm-all-right-Jack individualism seems to come with a side-order of "screw you" aimed at the poor and disadvantaged.

Backstage I have a beer or three with Compton, the band's 21-year-old guitarist, the son of a broken black mum/white dad home which he calls "a 2-Tone idea that didn't work."

Known as Commie to his friends, he's wearing a natty suit with strides which in the true skinhead tradition look like they've just had a ruck with his shoes. A thoughtful and sensitive soul, Compton is still troubled by the band's recent day off in neighbouring Mexico. The band had visited El Paso (which translates literally as The Gateway or The Step) and slipped over the border to dirt-poor Ciudad Juarez in the Chihuahua Desert. "I couldn't get over the idea of being a tourist in other people's misery," he says. "I saw things that turned my stomach. The extreme poverty. The beggars on the street, many of them blind or deformed. Okay, we have poverty at home but to see such squalor here, right next door to oil-rich Texas – it's so disquieting, y'know."

It's a clash of values as much as anything else. As well as the 'black gold, Texas tea', Dallas is a real estate hot-bed and a bankers' paradise. In near-by Mexico, wages are low, and dropping in real value while food prices rise, benefits are virtually non-existent. There's no sign of that changing any time soon and no-one I meet in Texas seems that bothered. As one friendly taxi driver tells me, "It ain't our fault the 'Cans screwed up their economy." No sir-ee.

Compton and I chat about the Royal Rasses and Prince Lincoln Thompson's own charting of similar deprivation not too far South in 'San Salvador'. Radical dub poet Linton Kwesi Johnson, the Jamaican-born sage of Brixton, helped open Compton's eyes to political realities in his teens, he says. "He brought reggae into a British context," Commie explains. "It was music for and about black kids born in Britain and there to stay."

Black, British and proud – with music to celebrate that in a way that the old Rasta singing about Ethiopia never could.

Compton is sold on every aspect of 2-Tone – the music, the ideals and the business plan. Opening the doors of a complacent pop industry to new bands and new sounds; giving talent a leg-up. Sounds punk enough to me...

NEXT morning I talk them into the ill-fated Southfork Ranch outing, which leaves us relatively subdued; reflective even. After all Dallas was the place they jeered the Sex Pistols, and killed Kennedy... and shot JR. Back on the bus, Pauline tells us about the packed, all-white truck stop that the band had managed to silence just by walking in together. When they finally got seated, the two waitresses on duty ignored them for a good fifteen minutes

and, true to form, only lightened up when they realised they were English. Alf Garnett lives on this side of the pond too, only it's more than likely that here he's packing a gun.

It seems strange, not to say absurd to me, to judge people you don't know by how much melatonin they have in their skin; but that, apparently, is how the world works.

For a while we travel in silence. Desmond relaxes by eating doughnuts by the dozen; the others sit back and pour over the copies of *Sounds* and the *Daily Mirror* I've brought over from England, except for Pauline who tries to lose herself in a smutty paperback, until that is Ross 'Gross Halfwit' Halfin decides to take her on. Not wise. "Why do you always look such a miserable cow in pictures?" he asks, with as much charm as a hung-over border guard with piles.

"Cos I'm a grumpy fucker," she replies equally sweetly.

Because of her medical background, the Troll brings up the subject of his genital warts. "My, you really are Gross, aren't you?" Pauline smiles, before taking the upper-hand and prodding him into purple-faced paroxysms of passion over UFO, at the time his favourite band, and our next assignment here.

"You're joking?" she scoffs. "You really enjoy heavy metal? Honestly? What, you really go to the gigs? Are you real? Can I touch you? You don't head-bang do you?"

Ross hits back with a jibe about women not liking hard rock because "you've got different brains from men...basically, a woman has got half of a man's mental capacity."

Pauline smiles. "I may have only half of your brain, dear," she says sweetly. "But I'm sure that you've only got half of what a man needs to keep a woman happy."

And with that, Pauline Black of Romford, Essex, achieves the impossible. She shuts up Ross Halfin for a good ten minutes.

SEVERAL plays of the Specials album later we arrive in Austin where the band is scheduled to do a meet-the-punters record shop stop before the gig tonight. The store stocks quality imports – even the Cockney Rejects album is here – and has been running a 'Best Rude Boy' contest with an aging Jamaican doing his Jah Russell Harty bit over the sound system. The winner is a dim looking youth who, in the style of the old 'On My Radio' advert is clutching a battered transistor to his left lughole.

The image is ruined only by the naff shirt he's wearing, with collars like Dumbo's ear-flaps.

"What do Rude Boys do?" he asks Pauline as he picks up his prize.

Exercising remarkable self-control, she smiles sweetly and replies: "I don't know; I'm a rude girl."

"Do they smoke grass?" the youth persists; producing a skinny little spliff that looks like it wouldn't get Atom Ant high. Pauline just nods, commendably swallowing a clear desire to burst out laughing. "Cool," the kid says, and he wanders off happy.

Another guy, older and fatter with halitosis and a Buffalo Bill goatee, turns up in a strange mishmash of black and white patched clothing. He looks like a deranged Music Hall turn. And he's loud. Buffalo Bullshit. Maybe his keepers had let him out for a few minutes while they clean his cage.

"It's just another uniform here," I say, thinking out loud. "They don't get it yet."

Neol Davies agrees. "Most of the country is like that. In LA especially, it's just a pose. Which is why it's good for us to play Texas, it's pretty much virgin territory."

Neol is 28, tall and ashen-faced. He describes himself as "probably the nicest person you'll ever meet." And it's probably true. Like all of the band, he has strong ideas of what The Selecter stand for.

"I'm really glad that none of this band has gone to art school," he says. "I'm not making a big thing of it but I just like the idea of none of us having gone through that process. It's just a feeling I have, an earthy feel."

We talk about class, and how even racial trouble often is more to do with class and culture than ethnicity. "The middle class ideal has real power, and a lot of people aspire to it," he says. "But over here it's much worse. There's a lack of good media. On the surface the USA is about choice but when you dig deeper hardly any ideas get across at all.

"Even in music, it takes so long for ideas to come through. Fashions aren't really important here, whereas in England they are, as they're a way of heralding a new movement. Here everything seems to stay stuck in the past. Prejudice goes back generations here. Segregation is a tradition, a voluntary apartheid – on both sides of the racial divide. The only thing we've got like that in Britain is religion in Northern Ireland; that mule-headed sectarianism. People stay separate. There's no cultural inter-change which is a real shame because I think it is people's differences that make the spark of living."

Charley Anderson is convinced The Selecter could help change that. "I think we could get across to the masses over here," the former electrical engineer says. "2-Tone isn't just a fashion. It's not a hip thing, it's a whole philosophy. We stand for people coming together socially whatever their race, creed or colour. And if we can help bridge those gaps in America, all this will have been worthwhile."

Admirable sentiments indeed.

The next morning I shake hands with the band after breakfast to go off and meet up with rock legends UFO. One of the bell-boys, a friendly kid who has been smiling to all of The Selecter's faces as nice as pie, sidles up to me and grins.

"You'll have a lot better time with UFO," he says. "There ain't any niggers in the band."

POST-SCRIPT: The Selecter never did conquer the States, neither did they harness their remarkable live energy into a lasting studio career. Their first three singles made an impact, but subsequent releases didn't do the business. Their fourth, 'The Whisper' didn't even go Top Thirty in the UK. Increasingly pissed off, the band split from 2-Tone and decided to change direction – Charley wanted to go heavier into reggae, Neol more into rock. There were internal problems too. During the long arduous US tour, the band had split into two clear factions with Charley, Desmond, Aitch, Commie and Gaps sitting at the back of the bus smoking ganja and listening to the kind of reggae Pauline would have called misogynist. Too much pressure. Desmond quit out of the blue and for good in August, and in the resulting power struggle Charley was sacked (by Pauline) two days later. The two of them went on to form the People who never meant a light – they released one flop single and then they were gone. They were replaced by a couple of white guys from the Pharaohs. The new band slowed down the former frantic Selecter pace, softened up, aimed to be more soulful…and still flopped. They recorded a second album, Celebrate The Bullet the following February. The title track was strong, a great atmospheric song, with addictive 'bendy' – apologies for the technical term - guitar flourishes.

I loved it. At any normal time, it would have been a good choice for a single, and a sure bet for the Top 20. Unfortunately, it came out just weeks after John Lennon had been gunned down by Texan fantasist Mark Chapman outside of the Dakota Building in New York City. The lyrics were clearly against gun crime ('Celebrate the bullet / Put your finger on the trigger / But you don't have to pull it...') yet the title alone meant an instant radio ban. It was the band's first flop. Poor album sales ensued. Pauline left soon after to pursue a solo career before coming into her own on the TV where she graduated from presenting kids show Hold Tight to serious / dull Channel 4 chat show *Black On Black*. She had acting parts in TV's *The Vice, Doctors* and *The Bill*, and played Billie Holliday very well, it's said, in a stage play. She was a tough cookie – she had to be, there were very few women on the 2-Tone scene. And she remains a Ska icon; loved most of all for those first three hits and her magnificent lungs.

I've not seen Compton for thirty years, but I'm sure he would have been chuffed about the scores of quality Ska bands that erupted in Mexico. Charley Anderson and his red locks now reside in Bogota, Colombia, where he works as a producer. Various reunions and versions of the Selecter still play to this day, but largely to middle age rudies reliving their glory years. It's all retro now.

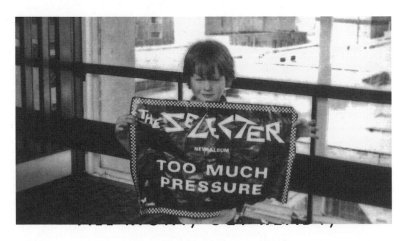

FRIARS AT THE MAXWELL HALL AYLESBURY

WED. MARCH 19

THE PRESSURE TOUR

THE SELECTER

THE BODYSNATCHERS

THE SWINGING CATS

TICKETS 250p FROM USUAL OUTLETS OR 250p AT DOOR (i.a.) MEMBERSHIP 25p

The Skinhead

JUDGE
DREAD

THE SECOND COMING OF JUDGE DREAD

Germany, December 1980

HERE WE GO...'

Judge Dread tells me to meet him and his song-writing partner Ted Lemon in "our favourite restaurant" close to Hamburg' infamous Reeperbahn; a nice place to go window shopping, by all accounts. Prostitution is not only legal here – it's celebrated. Even so, I'm a little startled when I arrive to find Dread and Ted at a table watching a black dwarf with an appendage as long and hard as a Polish surname servicing a large, willing and naked blonde. I hadn't anticipated that kind of starter. "It's the cabaret," the good Judge chuckles. "Look at the size of that!" He indicates the dwarf's proudest possession. "It's got everything except an elbow."

"What are you having, Garry?" asks jovial Ted. Not the coq au van, I say. And the air is cleared. We laugh, we chat, we drink, we eat; Dread drifts off occasionally and pulls a few peculiar dreamy expressions... and then something even stranger happens: a cute female dwarf, a red-head in stockings and suspenders, emerges from under the table wiping her mouth.

While we've been tucking in, the Judge has been enjoying an altogether different kind of nosh. "If that was a crime, she's swallowed the evidence," the ruling king of rude reggae remarks with a grin.

Incredible... I've been on the road with Steve Jones and Paul Cook, the

Damned, Max Splodge, Iron Maiden and Thin Lizzy, and yet it's taken an over-weight 34-year-old ex-bouncer from the sleepy Medway town of Snodland, Kent, to take my breath away.

It's like a scene out of a semi-comic porn flick, with dialogue to match.

"My aperitif," he shrugs.

"She had a pair of teeth?" Ted banters.

"Nah, she took 'em out before she started."

Dread notices that I'm looking a little surprised. "Do you fancy one, Gal?" he enquires with a wink. "Just ask for a 'short'. I've left my American Express card at the door. Whatever you have, they just charge to the old account."

"American Express," chortles Ted. "That'll do nicely." Maybe later.

"Great puddings," says Dread, studying the menu.

"36Ds I reckon," replies Ted. This ain't rock'n'roll, and it's not genocide either. It's more like Confessions Of The Rudest Rude Boys In Town.

ALEXANDER Minto Hughes, known to his friends as Alex, his fans as Judge Dread and his enemies as "that dirty old bastard", is enjoying his second coming (ooh-erh missus, etc) here in Germany on the back of the 2-Tone explosion.

The burly former nightclub doorman, bodyguard and debt-collector for Trojan Records became an underground legend in the early Seventies with his string of skinhead reggae singles: 'Big Six', 'Big Seven', 'Big Eight', 'Y Viva Suspenders'...all of them saucy, all of them banned by the BBC, and all of them chart hits. The dirty old bastard notched up two Top Tens, four Top 20s, and one Top 30. He then unzipped two more tasty 7inchers that pleasured the Naughty Forties. Sadly my personal favourite, 1978's 'Up With The Cock' ('Always asleep by ten o'clock, at six on the dot she's up with the cock' - about working on a farm of course), had fizzled out at a feeble 49.

"If it had been 69 we would have been happier," Dread laughs. His formula has remained unchanged since 1972's 'Big Six' (itself inspired by Prince Buster's far ruder 'Big Five', not to mention Verne & Son's 'Little Boy Blue'): simple effective reggae tunes married to nudge-nudge seaside innuendo ("That's an Italian suppository," wise-cracking Ted informs me.)

The madness starts as soon as I land at Bremen Airport. I'm strolling slowly through arrivals, more than slightly concerned by the number of stern-faced, submachine gun touting German plod about, when I'm knocked scatty by the kind of friendly pat on the back that would incapacitate a 25 stone grizzly bear. I spin round to clock the beaming face and comb-over barnet of Ted Lemon, Dread's portly, Pilsbury Doughman proportioned partner in rhyme.

The Judge himself is decked out like a minor league football manager, wearing a flat-cap, shades, and a ticket tout's fur over-coat. He is in the company of a young and willowy fair-haired fraulein, the two of them obviously joined together by more than a common faith in the future prosperity of the European Economic Community. After a lingering embrace, Dread drags himself away and shakes my hand as if he's trying to wring best bitter out of a house brick; and then, with a casual wave to the forlorn Teutonic temptress, we're off to Jah Lemon's waiting hire car.

"Well, that's me set up next time I'm in Breman, know what I mean Gal?" his legal highness guffaws, giving me a couple of gentle nudges in the rib department that would have put Big Daddy down for the count. "'Andsome or what? You wouldn't kick that out of bed for farting, would you, boy?"

We motor off towards Warstein and tonight's gig. In less time than it would take Mary Whitehouse to slag off a Carry On film, Dread is describing the many delights of Deutschland in the dirtiest of details. The great man is as happy as a dog with two dicks. It seems the world's second largest pop market has taken old Alex to its well upholstered bosom. He has enjoyed substantial second time around chart successes with 'Big Six' and 'Big Seven', not to mention his latest album 'Reggae & Ska', and prime slots on a couple of TV promoted compilations. All of which has made Judge Dread more of a star here than either Terry Hall or Suggsy. And consequently, a sex symbol. You read that right. Dread is getting as much bed-time action as Mick Jagger on an all-oyster diet. My mind is not the only thing boggling.

"We're not gigging as such out here," he explains. "We're doing PAs on the disco circuit. I just jump up and sing over backing tracks. It's cheaper than coming out here with the band, and the punters are happy enough. Big old venues too, some of them are 4,000 and 5,000 capacities..." That may seem unlikely enough, but there's more... Dread has, it would appear, also become a cult star among the German aristocracy. Proper upper class Krauts: barons, nobles, counts – I think he said counts.

"These big-wigs are bunging Dread a grand a time to have him perform at their private birthday parties," reveals Cockney Ted.

In Hamburg, at the Third World Club, one "little darling" coughs up £250 to reserve a stage-side table, and another £250 to persuade the Judge to do an extra encore. The extent of the ensuing after-sales service is best not referred to in detail in a respectable family publication.

But why? What can the German upper crust get out of watching a big English bloke with a beer gut singing about Winkle Trains and Doctor Kitsch with his injections? ('I push it in, she pulls it out/I push it back, she starts to shout/"Dr Kitsch, you are terrible/I can't stand the sight of your needle...")

"I can't really understand it," Dread admits. "Maybe because it's so down to earth and dirty they get turned on by it. Maybe it's a walk on the wild side for them. Or maybe it's like the way rich Yanks pay John Holmes" – a legendarily endowed porn star – "to turn up and screw their missus. Maybe now Dread's gyrating cock is fashionable.

"I don't really get the Germans at all," he goes on. "For a country that seems so permissive about what they let go on, they do strike me as being prudish. They don't like talking about it. I said to one promoter, 'Cor, I couldn't half do with a grind tonight' and he was really embarrassed."

We drive on, speeding south down the Fuhrer's autobahns towards Warstein, leaving behind countryside as flat as Olive Oyl's chest for picturesque villages, snow-kissed hills and woods. "Beautiful here innit," the Judge observes in a rare moment of pastoral reflection. "Lovely views. It's like driving through a Christmas card...Wouldn't it be good to get your cock sucked here? A wank in the Black Forest, that'd be something."

William Wordsworth himself could not have put it better.

Our hotel is a tranquil watering hole set in the slopes of the lightly forested Haarstrang mountain, slap bang next to a local nature reserve packed with bears, boars and other risky-looking critters. "I told the agency we liked wild night life," sighs Ted. "I might have known they'd get the wrong of the stick."

The place is warm and homely, attractively littered with the stuffed and possibly flea-ridden carcasses of deceased local mammals. "Taxidermy," observes Dread. "The only job where you can give an animal a good stuffing and get away with it." It's a mounting problem...

On the plus side the restaurant here serves the excellent local Warsteiner beer which is delivered to our table by a dishy blonde waitress who makes punk wild child Honey Bane seem flat-chested. The Judge is immediately smitten and wastes no time enquiring, "Kommen sie dahn the Papillion tonight, love? Frei! Gastliste!" A charming offer which the blushing busty beauty strangely declines.

"I think you offered her a free gasket," jokes Ted.

"She could blow my gasket any day," the spurned star replies. "She told me 'Nein', I think she guessed that's the length of my cock..."

THE Papillion Discotheque seems much friendlier. It's packed out with punters and boasts a fine array of lagers which we partake of liberally in the interests of tourism, diplomacy and international good will.

Dread has pre-recorded backing tracks with his excellent black and white British band back home. He divides his act into two half-hour sets, surprisingly mixing pop reggae arrangements of soft soul songs like The Tymes' 'Miss Grace' and 'Some Guys Have All The Luck' by the Persuaders, along with more familiar saucy standards such as 'Big Six', 'Big Seven' and a soupcon of Max Romeo's 'Wet Dream' thrust gamely into 'Rudy, A Message To You' – the Judge has been covering this 1967 Dandy Livingstone rocksteady original for years.

On stage, the big guy sports a fine pork pie hat and a double-breasted gangster suit; he performs like a randy Sid James at a Page 3 girl's wedding, ogling and leering, unzipping his fly, making vulgar gestures and frequent references to 'lieber-wursts' which roughly translates as love sausages. The audience loves every corny, horny minute. They're quick to dance, quicker to smile, and well up for singing along with the "Uh huhs", "right ons" und so weiter with a passion. There isn't a hint of trouble. "Refreshing," Ted Lemon points out, "when you consider how many of them umma louts they've got over here."

BUMBLING backstage a few beers after last orders, Ted and I are surprised (or maybe semi-surprised) to find the Judge engaged in, ahem, an intimate encounter with a busty, thirty-plus dyed blonde. The classy cracker smells like the perfume floor at Harrods and is weighed down with what looks like an entire shop window's worth of unsubtle jewellery. She offers Dread a lift home in her year-old Mercedes. Lucky old Judge! Talk about have gavel, will travel...

We decide to follow behind. Before too long the classy seductress pulls off into a woody side turning and the imagination doesn't exactly develop muscles working out what's going on. The windows are misting up, and is that a naked foot pressing up against the glass? Mein Gott!

'Ikki takka, tikki taka, dikki taka, tai ya, whoop ai-ya, pussy catcha fire...'

Ted and I decide to hang about, just in case. I'm no longer entirely sure in case of what, but I had had a lot to drink. It's just as well we do, though, because the local cops waste little time turning up at the scene of the grind.

Herr Sergeant is a proper charmer with a military cop's crop and nostrils as piggy as his eyes, a real loss to the Gestapo. He gives us a good mouthful of guttural abuse and is none too happy with our "Nein sprechen German, Herman, me old fruit" replies. He gives us a look we could have shaved with and trots off to the passion wagon where thankfully m'learned Judge and his bit of Prussian posh are now fully attired. Later we get the full story: it seems Frau Howsyerfather is something of a local dignitary – we suspect a married one - and the Aged Wilhelm were just looking out for her. So no harm done, and just the one "Don't forget who won the war" hollered at their departing backs. But not loud enough for them to hear...

A beaming Dread jumps in with us. "What a brahma," he declares. "I would have banged her on the bonnet, but it was a bit tatters, know what I mean?" We head back to the hotel hoping for afters. Once again, the Judge gets more than he is expecting. The busty young waitress from tea time is shyly hanging around outside his room. Suffice to say the old Dread bedsprings were ringing out an Ode To Joy way into the small hours. Some guys have all the luck, indeed. All the 'Donald Ducks' as well... Not that Dread's good fortune prevents him from rising at the crack of dawn ("Lovely girl, works in the Co-Op" – Ted Lemon) and dragging us both down for breakfast.

"Got to make an early start," he cackles as he lays into a gut-busting post-coital feast. With my head throbbing, and rings under my eyes so big my nose looks like it's wearing a saddle, I wonder what the German is for Alka-Seltzer while silently cursing the smiling star and the next seven generations of his offspring. But as he and Ted start to reminisce it's hard to stay mad at him. Dread has stories so rude they make Ozzy Osbourne seem almost puritanical.

There was the time at the height of his fame in the UK when two women came backstage after his Brighton show and claimed to have "come three times" during the performance. They then produced vibrators as evidence and invited the whole band to help them come another three times before the club shut. On another occasion Dread got outrageously drunk with a friendly stripper who insisted on giving him head on a bench in Trafalgar Square – the details of which only came flooding back when he came round the next morning with his flies still undone and "little Dread standing to attention under a thin layer of frost." Then there were the usual array of chambermaids who preferred to make beds from the inside; and to top the lot the Judge tells of how a national household name DJ once pulled "a right old dog" on the road and was entertaining her in a ground floor hotel room. Dread moved in to watch through a gap in the curtains and promptly fell backwards like a pole-axed ox into the fish-pond...carpus interruptus.

Back in the car, en route to Stuttgart, Ted Lemon is giving a running, pilot-style commentary on the journey, thus: "Good morning ladies and gentlemen, this is your captain speaking; we're cruising at around 70 miles an hour at a height of six inches. The

weather in Stuttgart is fucking horrible. Refreshments will be served shortly. Please return the air hostess to the upright position after use. Mesdames and monsieurs, je suis votre captain, nous sommes..."

Between giggles I ask who the pair rate as comedians. It comes as no surprise when they come back with Jimmy 'Kinell' Jones, the Cockney comic beloved by Iron Maiden and Status Quo, who inspired and heavily influenced TV's Kidbrooke-born comedy superstar Jim Davidson. Dread's rude repertoire has roots way back in popular culture. There are obvious similarities between the Judge at his best and the immortal Max Miller, who came up with rhymes such as 'When roses are red, they're ready for plucking/When a girl is sixteen she's ready for 'ere, 'ere...'

How far removed is that from the Judge singing: 'Little Miss Muffett sat on a tuffet/Knickers all tattered and torn/it wasn't the spider that sat down beside her/'twas Little Boy Blue with his horn.'

There are other obvious overlaps with seaside postcards, Carry On films and stag comics. Dread's humorous oeuvres trade in double meanings and dirty minds. And like his predecessors, he upsets the establishment. Judge Dread is the only person in pop history to have twelve (a dirty dozen) hit singles banned by the BBC. Yet most of his lyrics aren't explicit – there are no pricks or cunts, no fucks either. He's never effed and blinded like a Sex Pistol. "I think it's because we're the first people think we're the worst," Dread reflects. "Someone said to me the other day that the Ivor Biggun 'I'm A Winker' wanking song was as bad as my stuff, but we've never made a record that blatant. People associate me with Prince Buster's 'Big Five' but I've never released a song that crude either. I make humorous records. I don't release anything I'd be ashamed of. I couldn't do a song like Lloydie & The Lowbites did, 'Shitting On The Dock Of The Bay'." See, even the ruler of rude reggae has standards.

It still hurts him that his records were banned. "You hear far worse than what I do on the TV," he says. "When Benny Hill writes a saucy single like 'Ernie' they play it, but when we do just the same thing... it's like they put the knife in. It's not that I need the airplay, it's the principle. I've sold more than a million records all told, probably closer to two, so I'm entitled to go on *Top Of The Pops* and wave to the public, aren't I? Because the public is all I'm interested in. I'm not interested in the 'ego trip' of going on *Top Of The Pops*." He shakes his head. "They won't even let kids wearing my tee-shirts on the show," he says, adding "Prigs." Well it sounds like prigs...

Some critics, understandably perhaps, have called him a sexist, but you'd have to be a right prune to be seriously offended by his essentially puerile playground smut. Ted Lemon is less charitable. "Oh yeah, they're the worst, the feminists, the ones who come up, look down their noses and say, 'I don't like you'. Two hours later they've got their drawers around their ankles begging for more. It's always the way."

DANCE CRAZE

A simplistic analysis perhaps, but you'd have to agree that the image of a knicker-less Germaine Greer, for example, begging for a length of judicial helmet is a funny one. I tease Dread by asking if rumours (which I've spread myself in Jaws) about his good self and Bad Manners PR Sue Randy are true. "Nah," he laughs. "She wanted to, but I didn't want to spoil her for other men. Oi! Oi! Look at that bleedin' snow, Gal. If we got stranded out here they'd have to send Alf Martin" (esteemed editor of *Record Mirror*) "out after us with a barrel of brandy around his neck."

"You're joking, that bugger would drink it all," retorts Lemon, no doubt libellously.

Alex Hughes became an over-night recording star at the age of 25, nine years ago. Before that he'd been a professional wrestler under the evocative moniker of The Masked Executioner. He'd also worked as a minder for the Rolling Stones. He was a male model for a day; he fed crocodiles at London Zoo. He was a debt collector for Trojan Records until an axe in the head ended that chapter in his career. "I didn't even ask them to cut me in," he jokes.

Dread's music biz connections date back to the Sixties when he had worked as a 22 stone crop-headed doorman at the Ram Jam club in Brixton, where he first met Prince Buster, and the Flamingo in London's Wardour Street. He took the name Judge Dread from a Prince Buster song, but cites Laurel Aitken as an influence. "Laurel made a record called 'The Rise And Fall Of Laurel Aitken' which was a rude one, y'know, rise and fall - we all know what that means, we know what was rising, it wasn't Tower Bridge. I think he's the only one who ever made me think there's money in all this."

Alex was running his own reggae disco in South London when he began toasting 'Big Six', written by him and Ted, in the clubs. When the song was first released on the Big Shot label in June 1972, it sold 68,000 copies to the ethnic black audience pretty much immediately. EMI picked up on the distribution and it sold a quarter of a million in just over a month. Even when they released 'Big Seven' months later, 'Big Six' wouldn't drop out of the charts. It stayed there for six months, selling in excess of 300,000 copies without a single airplay. The single became an institution, like the Richard Allen books. Every council estate tearaway had a copy.

A stream of similar filth followed, of which all except 'Big Eight' which was apparently left off "by mistake" are available on Dread's brand new '40 Big Ones' compilation album. The Judge put more reggae in the UK charts than even Bob Marley. He began to fall from grace at the same time as the whole generation of glam rock stars, but like Slade and Gary Glitter, the big man was never forgotten and with the skinhead revival of the late Seventies so the Dread live audiences started to swell up (matron!) to a respectable size again.

"I'd been predicting the Ska boom for years," Dread says. "Remember it was 1975 when I wrote 'Bring Back The Skins'. The only things I frown on with the new lot are the sieg-heiling, which skinheads never did, and the violence, the way kids think they've got to go out and fight. I've always been involved with reggae music and I've never associated it with violence. Dread was the first white reggae hit obviously but now Bad Manners are carrying on that tradition. I think of Doug as sort of Baby Dread. I'm very pro that band. I like that type of thing. I like Madness too. But Selecter were too serious for me. Bad Manners are in it for a laugh and if you want to last as a band you've got to enjoy yourselves. The Specials are a different thing cos they were the first.

"I'll tell you what, I wouldn't half like to see the fat boy having a bunk up. I'd pay to see that. Imagine the state of him starkers, with that belly! He must have a little cock cos nothing grows in the shade. Of course, she'd have to go on top. And she'd still burn her arse on the light-bulb."

Dread goes on: "I love Britain obviously and I want to work back home again soon. Things like this tour are like a break for us. It's hard graft but it's relaxing. And everywhere is different. How many times can you go up and down the poxy M1? You get to know every bump on the road. I'm on nodding terms with the crows. Things like this keep you going because you don't know where you're going or what you're going to find when you get there. And obviously you've got to chase your ace. That's why I'm here. We're selling records here. Germany has become another Dreadland. Another couple of hits and we can bring the band over and do it properly and play the 10,000 seater venues. I want to play for the squaddies too if the NAAFI will book us."

Right now, Dread and Ted are working on a book and film project called Working Class Hero. Alex still sees himself as working class. "Dread was the first punk and I'll always be a punk," he insists. "I was saying bollocks and spitting and putting me fingers up when Johnny Rotten was still pissing his pants. I wasn't born I was hatched out by the sun. Someone had a wank on a window and I was there.

"The black people created a white reggae hero, a working class hero, and that's the way I will always be. I've never wanted a big house in the country. I've never wanted to lose my roots. And that's why it's great to see kids like Buster Bloodvessel making it. Working class kids, not stuck up idiots who think they're better than everyone else." He laughs. "Stinky Turner, the 4-Skins, what a great name that is. If the 4-Skins, the Members and the Gonads got together with The Slits there is no telling what would happen..."

'Oh she is a big girl now, oh she is a big girl now / She got fat and we know how...'

Sadly, although perhaps not unexpectedly, our conversation soon deserts the path of decency, with the Judge offering me insights into his relationship with prostitutes. "I'd screw a brass, but I wouldn't muff it," he says thoughtfully. And *Quadraphenia*: "That film got it all wrong, all that bunking that was going on at that party, that never happened. And no fuckin' proper Mod ever followed the Who..."

The last time I see Judge Dread is at Hamburg airport. He comes along to wave me goodbye but gets distracted by a petite and heavy-breasted brunette, who he chases after offering such romantic endearments as "Come now sister, lay some sweetness on I-man, bloodclaat..."

Ted Lemon looks at me and winks. "If you can't beat 'em, join 'em," he chortles. "And if you can't join 'em, beat off..."

Wise words indeed. And as tubby Ted wobbles off in hot pursuit a shocking thought occurs to me. I've been out here for the best part of a week and I've only mentioned the war once... I must be sickening for something.

BAD
MANNERS

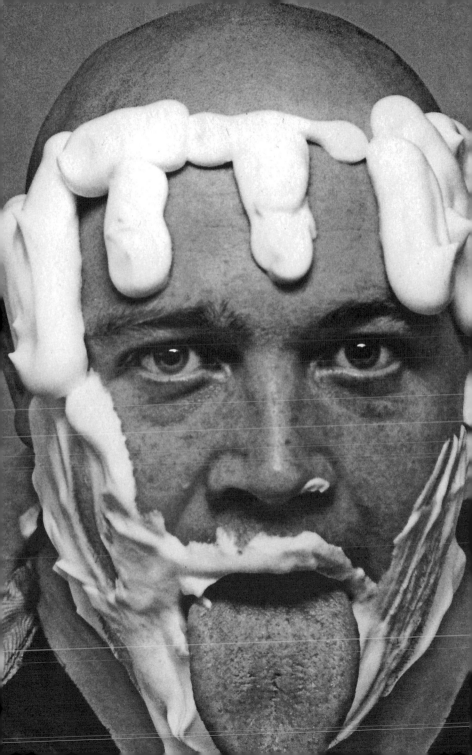

LIP UP SCATTY! THE HEIGHT OF BAD MANNERS

June, 1980

'YOU WON'T PRINT THIS WILL YOU? WELL I HAD DIARRHOEA FOR TWO DAYS – YOU PROMISE NOT TO PRINT THIS? – REMEMBER THAT WHITE BOILER SUIT I USED TO HAVE? WELL I WAS WEARING IT WHEN I HAD TO MAKE A RUN FOR THE BOG. EXCEPT SOMEONE WAS IN THERE, AND...' – DOUG TRENDLE. JUNE, 1980

THE SKA REVIVAL

I'm on the cramped Bad Manners tour bus, somewhere in the east of Scotland. It could be the low road, it could be the high road, there's no way of telling. The humour is low; the behaviour most definitely suggests high. This battered old van must be going close on 60mph and yet half of the merry mob of oddballs I'm travelling with insist on climbing out of the window and swinging up onto the roof rack.

What a bunch of ne-ne-na-na-na-na-nutters!

If that's not bad enough, in front of me Winston Bazoomies, the tousle-haired harmonica player, is swinging around like a demented gibbon with a clapped-out cassette player pinned to his left ear. It's blasting out the most eccentric mix of music this side of the Peel show: a chronic smorgasbord of sonic insanities ranging from Cajun pop to rasta-beat via Irish jigs, Creole zydeco and what sounds like Greek rockabilly – kebababilly? – that has lost its (Elgin) marbles.

"This is pirate music," he hollers. "Ahhh! Sing lad, Jim lad."

He falls to the floor, ripping his shirt in the process, but keeps on yelping, "C'mon boys, are you ready? Here we goooo!"

"HE has been like this since he was four years old," explains beefy Buster Bloodvessel, alias the equally beefy Doug Trendle, patiently. "He couldn't speak properly until he was about ten. He used to wander around Hackney saying things like, 'Papa beat me, and I have to go home for my tea', and 'Give me your false teeth and I'll eat your jaw.' He used to feed his sister leaves.

"One day me and my best mate, Eric Delaney, bowled round his house and found him screwing his mattress, no lie." Let's hope at least that it was well upholstered...and open coil. Doug pauses as if to consider the image, and then adds romantically "If sperm were rocket fuel, that mattress would have flown like an Arabian carpet."

Winston is of course the man who delivers the three-minute gibberish intro over the Magnificent Seven theme at the start of the band's set. The trouble is his lunacy is not confined to the stage. Already on this tour he's got the Bad lads and sometime tour support, Ska band Headline, ejected from a motorway cafe in Cornwall for giving a demonstration recital on top of a table. And he has frequently got them all ejected from warm guest house beds thanks to his odd habit of screaming "the world's loudest yelp" at unexpected moments.

BAZOOMIES seems to have crossed the line between eccentric and down-right section-able.

DANCE CRAZE

Bad Manners main man Doug is firmly on the showbiz side of crazy, though. The guy is so bald you can practically read his mind, and so fat he could moon Glasgow...and he uses his physical attributes for maximum effect. Not least his thirteen-inch conger eel of a tongue, which takes, or rather gives, some licking, eh girls? Most of the printable stuff involves challenges. Largely they're food and drink related, however backstage at Tiffany's in Edinburgh, I feel obliged to tip him off about another challenge being issued this week by the Jaws column in Sounds inviting his alter ego Buster Bloodvessel to wrestle someone in a proper wrestling ring; that someone being professional grapple giant Big Daddy, a man whose 24 stones make Buster seem almost slim.

Doug, who is a mere 18 stone ("19 with me steel-caps on"), isn't even phased. "I'll take him on if he's getting flash," Britain's biggest Ska star retorts instantly. "It is a bit worrying I suppose, he makes me look like Twiggy. But I'll wear me steels. He won't stand a chance. I doubt if he'll even turn up. Madness never did..."

Doug is of course referring to the ever-postponed Madness versus Bad Manners rugby match. "Madness can't get it together," he says, dismissively. "They reckon they're too busy touring, but it would have happened if they'd wanted it to happen. If you ask me they shit themselves when they found out we had three players who used to play for Middlesex and one who played for Kent County in the band. Suggsy in a scrum? Don't make me laugh."

Gene Simmons from Kiss never responded to that tongue measuring challenge either, did he? I say, stirring like Fanny Craddock on piece-rate.

"Nah, he's another one who bottled out," Doug sighs. "But I'd meet him any day. See, I reckon his tongue is probably longer than mine but it ain't as thick or as wide and I don't reckon he can move it at all, all he can do is stick it out. Not only is my tongue stronger but also I can do ballet with it. Look."

Without pausing to draw breath Doug pokes out his ferocious fleshy organ and gives a dazzling display: *Coppélia, Swan Lake, Cinderella, A Midsummer's Night Dream*, and an eye-watering *Nutcracker*... it's magical. He does it all, pirouettes, glissades, pas de seul, pas de basque – his mastery of oral choreography is beyond dispute. If that tongue could talk what a cunning linguist it would be.

Yep, I'd wager that Douglas would whip the arse of the sorry Simmons with the same ease with which he beat Judge Dread in the recent Battle of the Bulges in *Sounds* the other week. ("And Dread wore padded y-fronts for that," Doug divulges in mock horror).

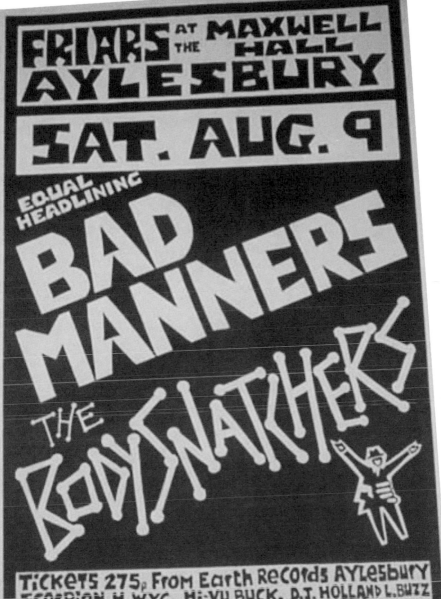

But of course the most effortless challenge of them all is the one Buster takes on in every performance with the band – turning a club full of passive punters into a sea of happy skankers.

At Edinburgh, the Tartan tickets aren't slow to succumb to those dance-happy ska'n'b rhythms...

BACK-TRACK several months to my first encounter with these lunatics. I was staying at a hotel in Coventry when this ginormous geezer rolled in wearing a shabby old crombie over-coat. The fat man had a ridiculous looking natty dread hat on his head that looked like John Bindon's willie warmer, and a great big cherubic smile on his face.

It was of course Dougie Trendle (born Douglas Woods). He strolled up to the pretty brunette behind the reception desk, winked, and, as bold as brass asked her "Would you like to come and see a band with a hit single tonight?"

"What's it called?" she asked, understandably suspicious. Doug took one step back, stuck out his massive chest and roared "NE-NE-NA-NA-NA-NA-NU-NU" at full volume. Then he stuck out his titanic tongue and pulled off the silly hat to reveal a bonce shaved as bald as a billiard ball. Everyone in the reception area dissolved into hysterics. The fat man turned and left the hotel, squelching his folds of quivering flab into a waiting taxi.

"Where was the gig?" I asked the girl behind the desk, when she'd stopped giggling.

"Warwick University," she replied, and starting tittering fit to burst again.

I had to see this. I jumped in a cab to the venue, talked my way backstage, and found a door with a sign on it which read simply 'Bad Manners – Keep Out.' How pleasant. But I was far too intrigued to stop now. I walked right in and regretted it immediately. The fat man was there with his eight other band members standing in a ragged semi-circle chanting nonsense. They waved their hands and patted their brows; they groaned, they grinned, they grimaced and they war-danced. It was horrific, blood-chilling; like a New Zealand rugby haka performed by the Goons. The colour drained from my face. Gentle reader, I had witnessed something few Englishmen have ever seen: the Bad Manners pre-gig warm-up ritual.

Then they pushed me aside and made straight for the stage. Buster stayed out of sight while the eight other loonies launched into a rich and brassily beefy Ska arrangement of the *Magnificent Seven* theme. That was my first experience of seeing Bazoomies acting like a man vaccinated with a gramophone needle dipped in mescaline. He stood there shaking and trembling as he mumbled incomprehensible nonsense into the microphone until Buster bowled on from stage left to roar: "SHADDUP!"

Eleven slices of luscious lunacy followed, intoxicatingly enjoyable enough to suggest that despite this being as late in the 2-Tone day as March 1980 and despite various smug pundits already talking dismissively about a "2-Tone bandwagon" and "worthless cash-in bands", Bad Manners were something a little bit special; real prospects.

Buster was inevitably the visual mainstay throughout the live performance, screwing up his face into agonies of anguish while toasting like a nutcase, pouring beer over his noggin, alternatively thrusting out his gigantic belly and revolting tongue at the crowd. But Buster also hit the only bum note here tonight, though, because at this stage of the band's career he was wont to periodically drop his jeans and flash the biggest and most disgusting arsehole you've ever seen at the blissfully skanking punters. Talk about Moon Over Miami, mes amis.

His chief rival for the eye-balls was the aforementioned Winston Bazoomies (born Alan Sayag), who would never stop moving, swinging his head and shoulders about with such jerky force that he was always threatening to shed his silly yellow sunglasses. Behind him was the more sober looking keyboard player Martin Stewart in his shirt and tie. Stewart, a hardy Scot, purported to be a former shepherd which possibly explains why the band's Hackney-born black drummer Brian Chew-It (actually Tuitt) always used to give him those worried sideways glances.

Then there was the brass section: Birmingham boy Andrew 'Marcus Absent' Marson (sax), willowy Gerry Cottle's Circus veteran Chris Kane (sax) and stocky trumpet tooter Gus 'Hot Lips' Herman. And that just left elfin bass player Reggie Mental, known to his parents as David Farren, and last but not prettiest, guitarist Louis 'Alphonso' Cook to complete the set. Louis always looked like he should be playing a banjo in Deliverance. He was more of a country bumpkin than a dapper Rude Boy, and had the strange habits associated with his kind. One Halloween night he broke into a coffin at Highgate Cemetery, pulled out a skull by its hair, and had a game of football with it... an image that brings a tear to the eye, not least of the poor desecrated corpse.

THE Bad Manners story begins with Buster. He was born on September 6, 1958 to single mother Lillian Wood in Hackney, East London, and although obviously he never went hungry, there was never much money about. The young Doug was adopted and raised by his great aunt Mary Trendle and her husband Edward – something he discovered by accident when over-hearing a conversation when he was seven. He had known his real Mum as Auntie Lilly, but he never knew his father (believed by many to have been the Michelin Man).

Doug started his musical career on the Arsenal North Bank, as a keen purveyor of football chants. His first official performance was in front of a magistrate after getting collared for "obscene singing" at QPR's ground. The doddery old Barnaby Rudge asked for a recital and even he had to laugh when "Who the fuck is Stanley Bowles?" wafted back full blast across the courtroom.

Former plumber Doug formed the first line-up of Bad Manners at Woodberry Down comprehensive school in Manor House, North London in 1976. They originally called themselves Stoop Solo and the Sheet Starchers. But they didn't start playing seriously until the summer of 1978. Over the next twelve months the Manners gang developed a style of their own. Like Madness, Manners were always more into fun and games and having a laugh than they were on social comment. Their chief distinguishing quality was an old-school rhythm and blues tinge, as exemplified by their Ska-ed up version of Sam the Sham's old 12-bar classic 'Wooly Bully' – a Pharoah hit for the Texan combo back in 1965. Which explains how they came to brand their music Ska'n'B. It was never particularly accurate, as the R'n'B was only evident in a couple of the songs they played. In reality, the Manners mainstays have always been big visual fun, the carnival brass sound, and a superlative blend of old Trojan favourites such as 'Elizabethan Reggae' and 'Double Barrel' which they interspersed with their own Ska-pop smashes. It was a mix that appealed to all sorts of audiences from skinheads to rugby clubs via pissed-up students.

Jerry Dammers saw them live in London in 1979, at about the same time as he first clocked Madness, and was impressed enough to offer them a deal with 2-Tone. It was probably sensible, in retrospect, that they turned him down. By signing with Magnet, no-one could realistically accuse Bad Manners of riding the 2-Tone bandwagon. The band's debut single, that great Mork from Ork reminiscent mutation 'Ne-Ne Na-Na' scraped into the Top Thirty in March, peaking at 28; and the follow-up 45 'Lip Up Fatty' made it to No.15 in the summer. It would take their third single, 'Special Brew', Buster's moving love song to tramp-strength lager, to finally get the

Manners boys into the Top Three where they belonged in September.

BACK in Scotland, in June 1980, I watched the band demolish another audience's resistance. But as Bad Manners take the stage, I'm surprised to notice a sudden outbreak of cropped haircuts among their ranks, with Alphonso, Hot Lips and Brian Chew-It all sporting shaven domes to match Buster's own. It makes the whole crew look like an off-shoot of the blubbery Fordham Baldies clan from hit US movie The Wanderers – especially when they are joined on stage by Bongo and the boys from the local skinhead battalion.

The film's man mountain terror (surely Doug's long-lost evil twin?) would have noted with approval that no-one "fucked wid da Baldies" this night. And a few music press pseuds would have been horrified to see even Hilary from 'cred' post-punk The Flowers dancing blissfully in the audience to the Manners' heavy heavy Munster sound. A good 250 happy punters were carried along by the "tatty tinkle of rude boy muzak" ((c) Dave McCullough) for an exhaustingly good eighteen song session.

The next morning, Martin Stewart takes over the van wheel for a hazardous drive to Aberdeen. I take shelter in the back with Doug and his pretty but petite girlfriend (again reminiscent of Terror's Tiny) who, at a humble seven stone 10lbs, inspires no end of unsavoury speculation about their sex life. Girl, you've got to carry that weight a long time...

As hipflasks of Scotch and spliffs circulate, Douglas suggests I partake of a little gentleman's snuff. Sadly it's not Peruvian in origin; but merely pulverised tobacco leaves for the snorting of. He proffers a box marked JH Wilson's Medicated Snuff for my perusal.

"It's very invigorating," he tells me, shortly before I sample it and then collapse, nostrils stinging, in a violent and protracted sneezing fit. "It clears the nose out, and it's really refreshing, don't you reckon?" My reply, mumbled and groaned from the floor of the van, is mercifully drowned out by a fresh blast of pirate music. But I think the word skanker was in there somewhere.

Unabashed, Doug relates some of the even more stomach-churning tour stories to date – confirming reports of a shotgun attack on their support band Headline at St Austell. "Yeah, luckily the bullet exploded in one of the suitcases," he says. "It just missed the keyboardist's head." The attack was apparently motiveless and the lunatic responsible has been charged.

Less seriously, Doug suffered a nasty attack of food poisoning

at Bridlington after polishing off a "bad crab whole." I wasn't even aware crabs had holes, but you learn something every day. The resulting 48 hour onslaught of the leaping Leon Trotskies is referred to in the quote at the beginning of this chapter. The boiler suit has since been burned, and its ashes scattered to the four winds.

Pausing only to salute the Bell's distillery as we pass, we pull off the main drag to visit Auchtermuchty, a quiet town in Fife made famous by John Junor's column in the Sunday Express as a bastion of ordinary opinion and sensible god-fearing folk. The stern no-nonsense Junor would certainly have invited Alice to pass her sick-bag if he'd known that keyboardist Martin Stewart had spent his formative years here allegedly "sheep-shagging" (D. Trendle) or perhaps more accurately shepherding for an elderly lady farmer.

We drop in for a refreshing eight pint breather in Martin's old local, the Boar's Head, where various family members have turned up to meet the band. While they make small talk, I take the opportunity to elicit all the boring old Actual Information that music paper articles are full of. This short Scottish stint includes a performance at the Loch Lomond festival; after that Bad Manners team up with Headline again to finish off the English tour dates. Next month they play a Finnish fest alongside Iron Maiden in front of 50,000 punters, which should be quite a laugh, proving

Buster doesn't eat Eddie or vice versa.

Their debut album 'Ska'N'B' came out in April and has gone silver. They're planning to record the follow-up, 'Loonee Tunes' in July for a pre-Christmas release; this is likely to include a couple of the live covers left over from the first album, like 'Tequila' and 'El Pussycat' as well as the expected bold and brassy originals.

I raise the subject of possible musical progression which provokes a Buster-sized ruck between Doug and Winston Bazoomies. Doug reckons they should move more towards "big band Ska" (sort of Laurel Aitken meets Billy Cotton at the Stoke Newington pie shop. The barking mad Bazoomies argues passionately in favour of swinging towards Cajun and general "pirate music". "You're talking out of your Arrrs," says Doug poetically.

Just to confuse matters further, Mr Alphonso puts forward an alternative scheme of doing a nine album long Ska interpretation of Wagner's Ring Cycle which would probably see them through until pension time; although knowing Doug he'd probably get stuck up, sorry, on Brunnhilde.

Out of the blue, a boozy Buster starts babbling on about an alleged "world anti-flab conspiracy", muttering darkly about the way Hollywood insists on hiring nice, slender heroes while baddies are generally portrayed by the over-weight. It's all a bit too predictable, so I'll interrupt his flow with a few amazing Bad Manners facts. Such as:

Their debut single 'Ne-Ne Na-Na' was not inspired by Mork from Ork's "Nanoo Nanoo" at all, but is actually a cover of an obscure number by a 1950s US combo called Dickie Doo & The Don'ts (actually the work of producer Gerry Granahan).

Doug nicked his stage name Buster Bloodvessel from the bus conductor character played by Ivor Cutler in the Beatles' 1967 film *Magical Mystery Tour*.

The band's rotund roadie Roy spends much of his spare time taping smutty stories from porn mags which he brings on tour as, ahem, educational entertainment.

And Brian 'Chew-It' Tuitt has a thing about fishes and little Asian women but, over-all, if pushed, would opt for little Asian fishes.

There is a lot more in this vein which it's probably best not to bother about. My note book from this tour includes progressively sillier nonsense from Bazoomies where he claims to have been an ant called Cedric in a former life, and rambles on about his next door neighbour painting his front door with a feather; but if you think the details are worth including you are probably as crazy as he is.

Back on the van, Doug talks at length about his hero Judge Dread, and his memories of skins years before at the Tottenham Royal (of 'Saturday Night Beneath The Plastic Palm Trees' fame – "dancing to the rhythms of the 'Guns Of Navarone"); the whole fascinating conflab stopping prematurely when stern Sounds snapper Virginia 'Fleshy Parts' Turbett insists on stopping the van for what feels like a ten hour photo session. This ends with saxophonist (and Harold Wilson sound-alike) Chris Kane getting hurled fully clothed into a lake.

"Don't worry Gal," roars Doug from inside a clump of ferns. "Next time we see you we'll have something serious to say about the state of the world as it is today, honest we will..."

Next time? NEXT TIME? AAAAAARRRGGGHHHHHHHH!

PS. THERE were several next times of course, but the one I wish I could remember more clearly was my trip to Germany with the lads almost exactly one year later. I can recall going to Hamburg with them, and Doug taking me along to his favourite Reeperbahn knocking shop (called Crazy Sexy) in St Pauli, the details of which are perhaps best left unexamined – much like a certain 'double oral' incident involving biker girls and chocolate sauce in Sheffield will be. Although I do like the fact that the German for bunk-up is bumpsen and when Hans needs the bumpsen Daisy, he knows exactly where to go to unburden his bratwurst...

I also recall Doug and the band breaking out into a terrace chant of "Two world wars and one world cup, England! England!" and the whole lot of us having to run what felt like the entire length of die sündige Meile (the sinful mile) to escape the wrath of locals who spoke English much better than we sprechened Deutsche. The police were involved but we still got to the gig in time – a huge open air festival with the Bad lads supporting the far more restrained quirky pop band Fischer-Z in Stadt Park. The lucky Krauts got to savour three brand new Manners masterpieces, all as breezy as a Winter's day on the Russian front, but none better received than the new single 'Can Can'.

THE best thing about the resulting spread in *Sounds* was that it came with artwork by Curt Vile better known to the world now as the genius Alan Moore of 'Watchmen', 'Swamp Thing' and 'V For Vendetta' fame. Alan/Curt only did two of these spreads – one for Bad Manners, the other for the Cockney Rejects. The Manners one was headlined 'The Deranged Doings of Desperate Doug... and his demented droogs!' It was basically a picture spread, with my captions, and Curt's graphics across the top. They were in British comic book style, with caricatures of the band, a running bottle of Special Brew, walking hamburgers, a guest appearance by Desperate Dan, and Buster in an unsoiled boiler suit carrying a particularly sexy, tackled-up 'Lorraine' under his arms.

The hits would keep coming for the world's maddest musical misfits at least for another couple of years. They released twelve singles of which only one, 1983s 'Samson & Delilah' failed to go Top 50. They had four Top Ten chart-busters – that summer's 'Can Can' went Top Three; 1982's 'My Girl Lollipop' (a gender reassigned version of Millie's 'My Boy Lollipop') peaked at No.9 – and six more top forty hits. Two of their first five albums went Top 30, three of them going silver.

In fact the only serious set-backs in the band's golden age were on the challenge front.

Doug was more than a little perturbed when some appalling health-obsessed quack made him abandon his greatest endurance test to date – eating more than 27 Big Macs (his record) in one sitting.

When word of that got out, Doug's reputation wobbled like his formidable gut. "Sod the doctors," he told me angrily. "The doctors told me to stop the eating contests but I'm going to have to keep on, just to keep my head above water.

"You know I met Chrissy Boy out of Madness in Stockholm and even he challenged me to an eating contest. I mean, Chrissy Boy!"

It was a shocker. And there was another one coming when Winston Bazoomies took on Chas Smash in a little-reported nuttiness joust which, although judged to be "a terrifying stalemate", left Bazoomies apparently "traumatized" and unable to tour. (Although thinking about, it that may just have been a PR story to cover the lovable lunatic leaving the band.)

At least Doug finally met Big Daddy, although to the best of my knowledge the actual bout didn't take place before the giant wrestling star, whose real name was Shirley Crabtree, died in 1997.

Bad Manners were always my favourite live Ska band. They turned every show in to a party. But my funniest memory from those early Munsterous Manners months came when Doug and

I were sitting in a hotel restaurant one evening in 1980. It was a rather plush place, full of snobs, but Doug couldn't care less. He took off his battered old black crombie to reveal a thick white sweater riding up over several spare tyres, themselves exposed to the world through a shirt riddled with holes the size of soccer balls.

Unsurprisingly the waitress couldn't stop herself from bursting out laughing. Finally, after several minutes of uncontrollable giggling she said, "Excuse me sir, would you like anything off of the sweet trolley?"

"No ta," Doug replied straight-faced. "It's fattening."

Priceless.

"What if your Mum could see you now," I asked him.

"You're joking," Dougie replied aghast. "She don't even know I'm in a band. She'd kill me. Nah, she thinks I'm working on a building site..."

And off he went back to the bar for another can of Special Brew, poking his tongue out at the toffee-nosed diners and wobbling ferociously.

Let's face it, after all that he just had to be a star.

FOOTNOTE: can I mention my one complaint about Bad Manners? Of course I can, it's my book. Only one thing they ever did annoyed me, and that was 'Can Can.' I found that single offensive. Not for prudish reasons, but for ruining one of my favourite historical fantasies. I mean, who of us hasn't imaged themselves transported 150 years ago, back to the Moulin Rouge at a time when Paree had never been gayer? You picture yourself on a discreet corner table, sipping wine and smoking a cheroot; to your left a demented midget starts drawing sketches like he's got no time Toulouse. To your right a barmaid gives you a saucy grin. The atmosphere is full of promise, of excitement, of amorous possibilities. By the time the artist is finished, you've downed a couple of bottles of house red and you're on the table shouting out for the governor to "Bring out the dancing girls..." The half-cut orchestra strike up the opening notes to that traditional big teaser the Can Can – a dance designed to raise up, um, trade for the brothel upstairs. Now you're punching the air in anticipation. Wave after wave of long-legged lovelies hit the stage, revealing tantalising glimpses of lacy smalls as they try and touch the ceiling with their toes. Look at all that flashing flesh – talk about the crumpet voluntary, John. From door to door it's garters galore. And COR, whose this femme fatale centre stage? Cop a load of those big legs, the big thighs, the even bigger beer gut... BEER GUT? What the f...? It's only Buster Bloody Bloodvessel in drag, his belly shaking like a plate of jelly in a wind tunnel as the wooden boards bend under his big steel-clad clodhoppers! And every man's interest wilts...That, my friends, is a dream deflated; that's a fruity figment of the imagination well and truly fucked. What a lousy rotten trick to play on the world. The fat bastard.

REVIEWS

2-TONE REVIEWS

THIS WAS THE FIRST EVER REVIEW OF THE SPECIALS AS THE SPECIALS. I WAS PRIVILEGED TO WATCH THEM OPEN FOR THE CLASH ON THEIR 'CLASH ON PAROLE' UK TOUR, LITERALLY FOUR HOURS AFTER THE SPECIALS HAD CHANGED THEIR NAME FROM THE COVENTRY AUTOMATICS.

THE CLASH/THE SPECIALS: FRIAR'S AYLESBURY

Garry Bushell, *Sounds*, July 8, 1978

FOR PEOPLE who like to put things in neat little pecking orders – and because of our conditioning there's a lot of them – the Clash are the Big Boys now, the punk establishment. Well, the Damned have split; the Stranglers aren't cool, are they? and with Johnny in cold storage the Ex Pistols are nothing more than Uncle Malcie's marionettes, mainlining on the puerile publicity of negative outrage. Jolly shocking, what?

Saddening more like. So, the mantle of 'leadership' falls unwelcome on the Clash, which naturally makes them an easy and obvious target for the facile bitching that often passes for 'informed comment' in certain sections of the music industry. Pete Silverton highlighted it all a fortnight ago... that not seeing them and the wait for the album had nurtured all that "they're finished/they were never that good" bullshit. So this, the first of the tongue-in-cheek Clash on Parole tour, was a chance to prove that all wrong.

And the message to the 1800 white men and women in Aylesbury
Friar's only looking for fun (and everybody else out there) is: don't
believe the media hyperbole, forget the 'fame', any group are as good as
they play. Do they make you dance? Question? DO something?

SURPRISE number one were support group The Specials (as they'd
been known for four whole hours. They were formerly called the
Automatics which was very confusing for the other Automatics, you
know, the 'when the tanks roll over Poland' ones). The Specials are a
five-piece multi-racial punk reggae group from Coventry, and the two
cultures don't so much clash as entertainingly intermingle. Whereas
The Clash play punk songs and reggae songs, The Specials ditties
combine elements of the two.

Yeah it sounds a phoney not to say disjointed formula but, surprise,
surprise, it worked. Song titles that stuck in mind include 'It's Up To
You', 'Dawning Of A New Era', 'Wake Up' and 'Concrete Jungle' which
give an idea of their stance even though I couldn't make out the lyrics
from where I was standing.

They finished on a nifty nostalgic version of 'Liquidator' and encored
with 'Naked' which sounded uncannily like Judge Dread's 'Big 8'
before racing up to an accelerating pogo-able pace and the final frantic

finish. Oi! Skin'ead, that ought to appeal to your sense of heritage. The Specials have been playing the West Midlands for a year. The vocalist sounded like Pete Shelley, the bassist's movements were a bit naff, but what the hell? They're competent, and enjoyable. Check 'em out.

THE KIDS had come for the Clash tho', and no one should have been disappointed. Tonight, they were the best I've ever seen 'em and this was my fourth time... twice before at the Finsbury Park stalag with its security goons and fixed seats, and once at Vicky Park where the sound system sabotaged the set. This time there were no goons, no chairs, an 1800 capacity crowd and dynamite sound. They kicked off with 'Complete Control', Strummer as ever shaking like a lunatic, and then it was a machinegun drum burst and into the first of the unrecorded songs, 'Tommy Gun'. Christ, no wonder they call Topper "the rhythm machine", his drumming gets better and better, solid, sharp building blocks for the others to construct the choones over. There were 16 songs tonight, half of them unrecorded, none of them substandard. In fact, the only shadow over the set was the crowd's conservatism.

A lot of the kids looked like last year's media images, right down to the swastikas, safety-pins and spitting, and it was obvious they really wanted the records churned out, and consequently didn't give the new songs the reception they deserved. New ones on me were 'Cheapskates' and 'All the Young Punks' ("This song is for punk rock which is the only thing that's happened in this country in living memory". Loud cheers). 'The English Civil War' is instantly accessible, based on the American Civil War song 'When Johnny Comes Marching Home Again'. Only this time Johnny's come on the bus and the tube, and this civil war's already started, see Grunwicks, Lewisham, Brick Lane.

Sure, The Clash are political, but there's a false dichotomy between their politics and fun. Clash politics aren't about being Boyson, Tyndall or Tony Benn, they're about living. Living is about surviving and having fun. Not about any electronic god or walking the dog. Not about passivity and acceptance.

That's why their politics are more convincing than Uncle Tom's. And that's why they hit me so hard 18 months ago when I was living on the sprawling wasteland the GLC call the White City Estate just a gob away from the throb, throb, throb of the Westway. Clash have always been best when they're trading on raw anger. Songs like 'London's Burning', 'Complete Control', and 'Capital Radio' are vitriolic power bursts seeping with gut conviction. 'Capital Radio' was probably their finest moment tonight. 'White Man In Hammersmith Palais' ("This one's no.32 in the charts – I'm so excited") is a really powerful anthem live, specially as Mick's solo was five times better than the studio version.

That "Burton suits / rebellion into money / Hitler" bit is a mighty two fingers to all that Thamesbeat media powerpap. What else? There was Paul at his best on 'Police and Thieves' (with last year's backdrops) which succeeded in turning the crowd into one heaving, seething slow pogoing mass. Mick over vocals for 'Jail Guitar Doors'; and 'Garageland' still sounds convincing even though the equipment shows they've long abandoned working in carbon monoxide fumes.

There were three other new songs which indicate there'll be no softening up on the new album either musically or lyrically. And finally, the crowd pleasing encores: 'I'm So Bored', 'Janie Jones' and 'White Riot'. All this and only the first night of the tour too! Enough to invalidate any lingering misgivings; as long as they still generate the sort of buzz of excitement you get when you skip off school for the first time at 13 they'll still be the Clash we know and love.

What more can a poor boy say? 'Cept perhaps to warn them not to play any more open air gigs. I hear there's a bunch of loose-boweled pigeons from *High Anxiety* just dying to get their own back.

THE SPECIALS: SPECIALS *****

Garry Bushell, *Sounds*, November, 1979

All you punks and all you Teds/National Front and natty dreads/Mods rockers, hippies and skinheads/Keep on fighting till you're dead/Who am I to say?/Who am I to say?/Am I just a hypocrite?/Just a piece of your bullshit?" ('Do The Dog')

THIS is the album that proves The Specials really are as special as our pumping purple hearts would have us believe. It's got the lot: the tunes, the exuberance, the beat, and the philosophy, god-dammit. This is an important record from an important band, a band that stands for something – and something a bit more than getting wrecking and shagging around.

There are fourteen songs on the Specials' debut album – five covers, nine originals. But each and every one of them is shot through with invigorating energy and irresistible excitement.

It's been a mighty long wait down rock'n'roll since their debut gig supporting The Clash at Aylesbury Friar's Club last summer, via Bernie Rhodes and the Paris debacle but it's been worth it. Some of the credit has to go to producer Elvis Costello, but we all know that the real kudos belongs to Jerry Dammers for making this dream happen and for having the brains to make it mean something.

Jerry's themes often boil down to a simple Oi, You, The Teenage Person Lurking At The Back, Think About What You're Doing. 'Just because you're a black boy/Just because you're a white/It doesn't mean you've got to hate him/Doesn't mean you've got to fight', run his lyrics on 'Doesn't Make It Alright.'

It's an attitude spelt out with perfect clarity in the album's opening track, Dandy Livingstone's sixties classic 'A Message To You Rudy' ('Stop your messing around/Better think of your future/Time you straighten right out/Creating problems in town...better think of your future/As you wind up in jail...').

Keyboardist Dammers credits 'Do The Dog' to Memphis soul legend Rufus Thomas but he's taken the song and twisted it like a pretzel until he could have almost claimed it as an original. Jerry's '(Dawning Of A) New Era' continues the friendly hectoring which feels close to lecturing on 'Too Much Too Young': 'You've done too much, much too young/Now you're married with a kid/When you could be having fun with me.' It's friendly advice – don't waste your life – delivered by a mate with a marked anti-social streak: 'Call me immature/Call me a poser/I'd love to spread manure in your bed of roses...'

Musically the album sounds sparse but as tight as an assassin's garrotte. The Specials are now a seven piece with brass supplied by Dick Cuthell on flugelhorn and trombonist Rico Rodriguez who by coincidence played on the 1964 original version of 'A Message to You, Rudy'. Horace's bass-playing gives the whole enterprise pace; the guitars are simple but effective; the vocals a mix of scowling punk and howling rude-boy.

All of the band's originals are by Dammers except for the short, sharp 'Concrete Jungle' – a phrase taken from Bob Marley's Catch A Fire – which was written by Roddy Byers, aka guitarist Roddy Radiation. There isn't a duff track here. Even the live highlight – the band's cover of 'Monkey Man' (a hit for The Maytals in 1969) loses none of its sweaty enthusiasm in a studio setting.

This album married clear and glorious echoes of the past (Toots, Prince Buster, Lloyd Charmers and The Skatalites) without ever sounding naff or retro-escapist.

We know the formula for the Specials success: old-time Ska meets today's punk attitude. We knew it worked live. What we didn't know was how good it could work in the studio; how it could turn out to be the soundtrack to life in decaying modern Britain.

Other bands have tried to combine reggae and punk before – from the rowdy Chelsea Shed singalongs of the Members to the classier driving power of The Ruts. (Fuck the Police!) But none have got the formula as right as the Specials have.

THE SPECIALS: MORE SPECIALS ✶✶✶✶✶
Garry Bushell, *Sounds*, September 20, 1980

TO BET or not to bet, that is the question. Whether it be nobler to sit pretty with a winning formula or take a gamble and walk on the wild side a jot...

It's stick or twist time for the Specials and if 'Stereotype' tipped us the wink that Dammers and co were into living dangerously it certainly never girded our loins for the extent of the change embodied by this brave new whirl.

The front cover gives the game away. Out goes the puritan black and white world of Tonik suits and stares soaked in sullen defiance and in its place there's a full colour snap of the band relaxing in casual clobber and smiling over a table full of booze. All very symbolic of the musical changes herein because the stark and direct punk-ska that characterised the early Specials and that was captured convincingly if not perfectly on the debut album has grown into a distinctly odd but surprisingly successful sound kaleidoscope that mates the band's essential dance beat with huge dollops of Motown pop and even huger dollops of trad Middle Of The Road music.

'Lounge Music', is how the band paint the new choons, 'muzak for the Eighties', and though self-styled intellectual critics will claim the band are working in areas previously explored by bald bores like Brian 'Earache' Eno, those in the know will suss that the true inspiration for this weird and wonderful move are obviously the legendary Edmundo Ross, the pioneering populiser of Latin-American rhythms, and even, don't mock, Billy Cotton Senior, the revered godfather of oi-oi music.

I must admit on paper the whole idea appears to suck a John Bindon-sized one but 'Stereotype' itself with its cossack choir boys and Come Dancing rhythmic setting for a tale of teenage tragedy illustrates how well Dammers' ambitious new bent can work.

The Big Bill Cotton spectre is raised on the first track, an infectious up-date of the centuries old Magidson/Sigman 'Enjoy Yourself' (believed by experts to pre-date even Juliet Devie) with its People's Pub Party 'have a good time while you're young' lyrics. And amazingly the band transform it into a real joyous jaunt chocker block with carnival brass c/o Rico and Dick and brightened up no end by Tel's sardonic "Hello I'm Terry and I'm going to enjoy myself first".

But just in case you misinterpret this as a plea for alcoholism as the only solution, the next number 'Man At C&A' turns the lyrical sten gun back on such social evils as the threat of world war and nuclear suicide, a juicy pop-reggae setting housing the catchy chorus: 'I'm the man in grey/I'm just the man at C&A/And I don't have a say/In the war games that they play.'

Next up are a couple of non-Dammers numbers. Roddy Radiation's 'Hey, Little Rich Girl' is bouncy, melodic and outrageously strong pop not to mention a tear-jerking tale of a snooty provincial filly fleeced by a flash capital city conman. And that's chased by lovely Lynval Golding's mellow top-skanking inclined treatise on apathy called 'Do Nothing'.

Then JD presents one of the finest frolics of the new set, 'Pearl's Cafe', a breezy insight into the horrifying depths of the human experience introduced by Sooty Show xylophone. This absurdly catchy swing-along number concerns a washed-out washed-up middle-aged boiler (portrayed by Bodysnatcher Rhoda – I make no comment) tempering moans about her unhappy existence with this Bertram Russell type philosophy – 'It's all a load of bollocks – and bollocks to it all.'

And that leaves Side One to end with a cover of Rex Garvin And The Mighty Cravers' gold soul oldie 'Sock It To Em JB' replete with punchy brass, machine gun drums, and James Bond film titles that's guaranteed to induce demented cursing from real soul experts and ageing Black Music founders everywhere.

Side Two kicks off with the single that segues into Neville Stapleton's 'Stereotypes Part II', a toast to a gent with vinyl veins content to while away his time with his stereo and callie weed. Roddy's ultra-odd 'Holiday Fortnight' comes next, an instrumental soundtrack for a spot of hols on the Costa Packet, its cheeks flushed with Spanish flavouring and Mediterranian allusions that conjure up vivid visions of sun cream squirted over puffy raw swollen purulent flesh and tiny emaciated dagos with nine inch hips and bloated fat tarts with their hair greased back presenting flamenco for foreigners (Cont Spanish Tourist Board).

The wretched Rhoda returns to join Terry for a tender ballad called 'I Just Can't Stand It' which presents the pair as the Pearl Carr and Teddy Johnson of 2-Tone over more Edmundo Ross influenced rhythms, This number features the amazing technical feat of having their voices coming out different speakers which means a quick flick of the balance control can eradicate the chanteur of your choice. And it ends with a romantic 'Goodnight Terry' 'Goodnight Rhoda' – definitely a Peters and Lea for the nineties.

'International Jet Set' is even weirder than what has gone before being much more obviously 'lounge music' with Terry's voice sounding unreal and alienated as he observes the jet-setters around him over the muzak – 'they all seem so absurd to me – like well-dressed chimpanzees'. And after that oddity the album climaxes with a plodding reprise of 'Enjoy Yourself' that conjures up pictures of bawling drunkards staggering out the pub doors well after closing time.

In general More Specials is a massively successful gamble, wider, warmer, weirder and as good if not better in its own way than its predecessor. For me it helps rout fears about the health of the 2-Tone cream which seemed to be losing momentum and impact over a criminally lax summer (what sort of youth cult packs its bags during the school holidays?).

And it also breaks down restrictive musical barriers and injects new life into a movement seemingly imperiled of late – what with Selecter appearing to fall by the wayside and a whole host of lesser artists threatening to topple 'the bandwagon' over.

With this and new and more adventurous albums in the pipeline from Madness, the Beat and Bad Manners the 2-Tone flag as both the danceable alternative and the positive end of skinhead thinking is firmly and proudly hoisted again.

The future isn't 2-Tone, but 2-Tone and son of 2-Tone records like this will continue to be a vital part of our future.

BAD MANNERS: BAD MANNERS *****

Garry Bushell, *Sounds*, April 5, 1980

OH DOCTOR I'm in trouble (well goodness gracious me), not only have I forgotten the rest of the words to the Peter Sellers/Sophia Loren teen aggression anthem I just cleverly opened this review with, but also I keep giving these Ska bands five star album reviews.

I try not to, but I just can't help it. When you're in an office where the sombre sounds of Kevin Coyne, Rush and the Pop Group pollute the air whenever your back's turned a record like this is a real life-saver. It's alive and it's a laugh, it makes you grin and gyrate through pathetic impersonations of Chas Smash dance routines and it's almost like Fatty Doug is poking his gigantic tongue out at the greyness and grimness of all that old man's music and saying bollocks pal, this is today's pop music.

And he's dead right. On this debut album Bad Manners take on Madness in the loony tune nutty dance stakes and almost win (gaspo!) with a pleasing pot pourri of farting frolicsome brass, singalong songs, and juicy skanking dance music, a little bit London, a little bit Ska Intensified, a little bit rhythm and booze, the whole lot christened Ska'n'b and guaranteed to fulfill Fatty's deepest ambition – to make skinheads, weightwatchers and other loonies get down there on groove manoeuvres and shake a dirty DM till chucking out time.

The r'n'b element is the thing that distinguishes Bad Manners from their partners in ska-crime and there's a tinge of it on most of the twelve numbers here but mostly it shows in the cover versions of old pub rock faithfuls 'Wooly Bully' and 'Caledonia' which show their roots dear, but are fine anyhow, especially 'Caledonia' a beefed-up rendition of Louis Jordan's big-band-r&b jump blues faithful which positively reeks of 'Happy Days', bobby sox and pony tails.

In all there's five covers on the album but you can't really knock 'em for that. Madness had four, Selecter five, and the Specials five plus a couple featuring 'musical quotations', so this is par for the course and like their contemporaries the mighty Manners stamp the covers with their own style so well that they are becoming almost self-defining.

Clancy Eccles 'Fatty Fatty' is the prime example, a totally infectious singalong that alongside their own 'Lip Up Fatty' manages to capture the fatty dread side of their considerable appeal. 'Lip Up Fatty' is probably a better song with Fatty sounding a touch like Nick Tesco as he analyses the basics of said slimming club spin-off: "Moving with the rhythm, sweating with the heat, moving to the rhythm of the fatty beat". If this is the next single it'll be Top Twenty, and I'll have a pony on that, Patricia. (Eh? – Veterinary Ed)

Elsewhere we get a rip-roaringly silly run through the 'Magnificent Seven' theme, possibly the finest western theme music from one of the finest Westerns ever made, and the whole affair reeks of silliness with Winston Bazoomies chattering away like a loony throughout. Three of these chaps hog the excellent brass section so I won't name names, but together they come up with a genuinely happy noise that sounds almost Mexican on some numbers, and makes you smile all the way.

'Ne-Ne Na-Na Etcetera' should be in the Top Thirty by now and if you ain't heard it you must be living in a cave, or Carnaby Street as it's sometimes known, and woops, I just remembered they also do a version of Bobby Picket and The Crypt Kickers manic 'Monster Mash' smash. And there's 'Scruffy The Huffy Puffy Tug Boat' which sort of defies description, more lunacy in 'Here Comes The Major' and 'King Ska/Fa' and a couple of departures from the norm in the tender love song 'Special Brew' ('Gonna spend all my money on you') and the more serious, atmospheric 'Inner London Violence'.

On the whole, though, the album comes across as one huge danceable party replete with funny noises and bouncing beats that show the nine nutters up as real prospects as opposed to cynical conmen. Given a choice between the Rolling Clash, Rush or Pink Teardrops In A Dark Ratio, I'd choose Bad Manners every time. There's just something about them, how can I put it, they make my heart go bom-diddy-bom-diddy-bom-diddy-bombombom. Goodness gracious, how contagious, goodness gracious me.

THE BODY

SNATCHERS

LIVE INJECTION: THE SCARIFYING RISE OF THE BODY SNATCHERS

THEY CAME FROM BEYOND THE STARS. STRANGE ALIEN CREATURES THAT TOOK ON HUMAN FORM, BUT WERE FAR FROM HUMAN...

'The Invasion of the Bodysnatchers' proclaimed the posters, 'the first seven piece all-girl and beat band in this Galaxy.' It was a cunning move. Fiendish in its simplicity: be upfront about your ploy, paint it as some kind of a joke and then maybe nobody would see through it.

To fool humanity, the aliens had assumed the guise of head-turning, and on occasion stomach-turning, earthling females.

Each of the magnificent seven had bodies worth snatching, and snatches worth...no, I don't know where I'm going with this either. Anyhow, they looked like everyday people you'd see in the streets. They could be your friends, your neighbours, your loved ones.

It was only when you got close to them that you realised that you realised how sinister, disquieting and dangerous they were...

Leeds, February, 1980. I'm at my hotel, minding my own business when Neol Davies (another obvious alien – he can't even spell Noel) booms out my name in a horrendous mock-cockney bellow that sounds like Derek Jameson having his head boiled in a vat of steaming hot eel liquor.

This sparks off an explosion of obviously over-excited female cackling and shrieking. I ready myself for the now customary assaults of lady admirers that have become the bane of my life, but instead I am caught off-guard by a vicious blast of water connecting with my left temple followed by a small plastic missile bouncing off the base of my spine.

It is my first close encounter with the demented, other-worldly horde that calls itself the Bodysnatchers. And if this is their way of saying hello, remind me to duck when they say goodbye.

At this stage I still believed they were what they seemed: human females, and as nice a bunch of women as you could wish to meet this side of the Soviet Tanks Corps, stranded without rations in Afghanistan.

There are, I discover, seven Bodysnatchers: singer Rhoda Dakar, bassist Nicky Summers, drummer Jane Summers, schoolgirl sax player Miranda Joyce, keyboardist and freelance illustrator Pennie

SINGLE O

LETS DO
ROCK STEA

CURRENTLY ON TOUR WITH THE SELECTER

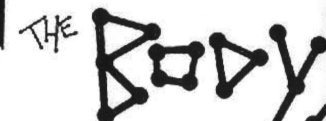

THE BODY

Leyton, rhythm guitarist Stella 'Scunthorpe' Barker, and lead guitarist SJ Owen, the 'SJ' standing, according to my unreliable notes for 'Sultry Jezebel', or possibly 'Steamy Jiggler'.

If you believe their cover story, the band got together in London last year after Berwick Street fruit and veg market trader Nicky caught the Specials live at the Moonlight Club in West Hampstead and was blown away by their Ska-tonic sonic assault.

She placed an ad in the music press, stating 'Rude Girls Wanted.' Not smart. "All I got at first were a load of dirty phone calls and filthy suggestions," she moans, as if surprised – indicating a basic lack of understanding of human nature.

Eventually Nicky put together a basic four piece, out of which the current line-up developed organically.

The Bodysnatchers made their first public appearance at London's Windsor Castle in the Harrow Road last November – just three months ago. After their second gig, various easily swayed male members of the Selecter asked them to be their support on the tour known to the public as '2-Tone 2'. By their fifth show at the 101 Club in Clapham, south west London, it seemed as if every A&R man in London was in the audience, along with such notables as Madness producer Clive Langer and Sire Records bigwig Seymour Stein.

They were so raw at this stage, saxophonist Miranda didn't even know what notes she was playing! When she was sober! Yet in the weeks that followed the Bodysnatchers had been signed up to the 2-Tone label. And their debut single – a rather fine cover of Dandy Livingstone's 'Let's Do Rocksteady' backed with the original song 'Ruder Than You' – will be released next month.

How could all this be happening so quickly, if not by some Machiavellian design?

You might cite bandwagon-jumping by the record labels and the media or the novelty factor of seven girls skanking rather than the usual hairy-arsed blokes but to me that sounds frankly naive.

There was some opposition in the collective 2-Tone camp to the band being signed. Surely, the critics argued, the girls were too inexperienced (as musicians) to be worth taking a punt on? After all 2-Tone's reputation rested on each release making it; and an already cynical music press were already eagerly waiting for Dammers and co to fail. Yet all of that sensible logic was swept away, as if by magic; and here they are, with a hot 45 ready in the pipeline.

THE SKA REVIVAL

How so? How was this even possible? It's not so hard to figure out, once you factor in the mind control...

I DON'T when exactly I first saw through them. But my suspicions were aroused last month (in January 1980) when they infiltrated a Mod Mayday down at the Bridge House in Canning Town, East London, and wasted no time eroding the hardened resistance of the assembled Mods and Glory Boys. Their rocksteady beat was tightening up nicely – the 'girls' had chosen a slower form of reggae than 2-Tone Ska to disguise the fact that they weren't the greatest musicians in this world, or their own.

Their set was mostly covers to begin with: 'Monkey Spanner' (originally a hit for the brilliant Dave & Ansel Collins), 'OO7 (Shanty Town)' which had been a smash for Desmond Dekker & The Aces, the aforementioned 'Do The Rock Steady', Booker T's 'Time Is Tight' and a reggae version of 'London Bridge Is Falling Down' – no doubt one of their apocalyptic goals.

The girls all claim to have human parentage. SJ's old man is also her bank manager. Market trader Nicky boasts that her dad was "a spiv" in the George Cole mould. While Miranda reckons her father still gives her pocket money. ("And baths" – Gross Halfwit). Rhoda insists that her Dad is called Rudi and is "the oldest West Indian in London - he's been here since 1926, when he used to drive a Model T Ford." Rudolph Dakar she asserts is a singer, who's also been a chiropodist, and the manager of the Caribbean club.

The name Bodysnatchers had no sinister connotations, claims Pennie Leyton. "It's body-snatching music, plain and simple. You hear it and your body can't sit still."

PS. The Bodysnatchers' only controversial song, 'The Boiler', was later released as a single by Rhoda with the Special AKA and promptly banned by the BBC. For Rhoda it was about feminism as much as sexual assault, the way women are perceived in society. The grammar school educated singer says "The Boiler was written about an attitude to women and to rape, an attitude that comes as much from women as it does from men, unfortunately. The kind of woman who won't tell her boyfriend's mates that she works and doesn't want them to know that she's more successful than he is. Feminism has got us jobs, but it hasn't changed our home lives enough yet. It hasn't changed our attitudes.

"Most of the 2-Tone bands were cool. But when The Bodysnatchers began playing with normal groups you'd hear men say things like

RHODA

THE SPECIAL A.K.A.

RICKY SIMMERS

SINGLE OUT NOW

c/w THEME FROM THE BOILER

'Do they really need a soundcheck? They're only girls'."

Now, here in Leeds on the 2-Tone 2 tour I find myself watching them in a haze that suggests that either I'm very drunk (And how likely is that? The very idea!) or that they're already messing with my head.

All I remember from the gig is cocky singer Rhoda swaggering round the stage, grinning and cheeking the crowd: "'Ere you'll get what you're given and like it mate!" (Rhoda works at the Brixton dole office where I suspect that's her catchphrase).

She has got a great voice, that's for sure. It sounds like it could have been manufactured by cunningly taping all of the great Tamla Motown girl groups of the Sixties, mixing them together and distilling them into one apparently human falsetto through fiendishly advanced technology.

I also remember there being just two original songs in the set. One is 'The Boiler' (about a sexual assault, so not so chirpy); the other, 'The Ghost Of The Vox Continental' probably makes a lot more sense the nearer you get to Alpha Centauri.

And oh yeah, I also recall Chelsea-supporting vocalist Rhoda opening the set with a cry of "This is the invasion of the Bodysnatchers" – as blatant as you like, before Penny threw in a saucy soupcon of Bach that led directly into '007 (Shanty Town)'.

Back at the hotel, I watch them take over a dark and dodgy disco in the back hall and electrify the bored drinkers, effortlessly enticing them out of their chairs to join in with their non-stop foxtrots and loony nutty trains. Come dancing? Some of the old fellows look like they might. (It's all a damn sight livelier than the sub-Jess Yates cabaret in the hotel proper. That only needs a few extra corpses and some Cliff Richard records to feature on one of those mogadoned Sunday evening religious chats with Lord Longford.)

The next morning I sit them down for a proper interrogation, asking them all the tough questions about their origins, philosophy and physiology. I tape every word, and write it all down as well...and yet as soon as I check it back on the train I realise that the tape is as blank as the pages of my notebook.

How could this have happened?

Thinking back, I could remember Rhoda being enigmatic and cheeky, and sassy fashion lecturer SJ being scintillating but as for their actual words, I could not recall a thing. I became scared, gentle reader. And I became even more scared as I watched their subsequent career develop. Their debut single, 'Let's Do Rock Steady' went Top Thirty and suddenly they were everywhere. On *Top Of The Pops*, on So It Goes, on Tiswas, doing Peel sessions... And they're good. They're getting away with it. I've even started to think of them as people.

THE WORLD'S FIRST SINGING MAGAZINE

FLEXIPOP

FREE SELECTER RECORD

No.1 60p

SPECIALS

JAM

BOW
WOW
WOW!

U.F.O.

BAD
MANNERS

WENDY
WU

THE
BEAT

BEAT ON THE BRATS

'TAKE HIM TO THE DISCOTHEQUE AND TAKE HIM TO THE PUB/ TAKE HIM TO A BLUES AND THEN YOU PLAY HIM A RUB-A-DUB, EHHH!

'MAN SAY YOU SHOULDN'T REALLY FIGHT; EACH AND EVERY DAY I WALK THROUGH THE STREETS AND I SEE MAN AND MAN GWAN KILL EACH OTHER 'COS YOU ARE BLACK AND YOU ARE WHITE/SO WHAT'S THE USE IN FIGHTING...?'

'DOORS OF YOUR HEART' TOAST BY RANKING ROGER

THE SKA REVIVAL

In the great Parthenon of 2-Tone heroes, The Beat always seem to be the hardest to define. The Specials are the pioneers, of course; Madness are nutty, Bad Manners are jolly, beer-guzzling loons, The Bodysnatchers are girls, The Selecter are the Ska band most likely to scowl and snarl... and The Beat? They're written off as the other ones; "the ones from Birmingham."

For a band who pushed very close to Madness and the Specials in terms of singles sales, sticky panties and teeny-bop acclaim, The Beat have generated nowhere near as much critical acclaim. That can't just be because of the Brummie accents, surely?

When they first broke through, the Beat were like Magazine - gleefully shot at by both sides. Roots reggae purists claimed that the band's teenage toaster Ranking Roger was just "ripping off" pioneers like the great Lester 'Cocaine In My Brain' Bullock, known to the world as Dillinger – although you could argue that he was just popularising their style. (The purists neglected to add that Dillinger himself had been hugely influenced by U Roy, Big Youth and Dennis Alcapone, even performing as Dennis Alcapone Junior at the start of his career.)

Other whiter critics complained that the Beat were dull, accusing them of being "bland" and "anonymous". An accusation which like much of the accumulated music press cynicism was cut to shreds when the Beat, from Birmingham, went on to notch up five hit singles with their first five releases, four of them Top Ten.

Ska-fusion hits like 'Mirror In The Bathroom' and the addictive 'Hands Off... She's Mine' showcased a delicious, delirious and highly individual blend of supple rhythms, sparkling choppers and radical pop.

I mean, come on, 'Stand Down Margaret'? How the heck can you call a song like that bland, dull or anonymous?

In the process of becoming Genuinely Famous, Ranking Roger and his handsome sidekick, vocalist and guitarist Dave Wakeling have become the fresh-faced pin-up favourites of a million adolescent ravers.

Singer, song-writer and all round nice guy Wakeling had tried his hands at most things before he formed the band. He'd been a fireman, a bingo caller, a lifeguard and a brickie. But it was while he was making solar panels on the Isle of Wight with his mate, and future co-guitarist Andy Cox that he met the only non-Midlander in the band, bassist David Steele (aka Shuffle) who they eventually persuaded to up sticks to Brum.

Slowly, the Beat was born. Wakeling came up with their name, simply by finding Roget's Thesaurus entry for 'music' and glancing through the long list of associated terms until he spotted the one he liked.

They started jamming together in 1978, but didn't actually play live until March '79 by which time they'd recruited reggae drummer Everett Morton who'd met Dave Steele when they were both working in a Brummie mental hospital.

'Black punk' Ranking Roger must have seemed like an asylum escapee when he first jumped on stage with them unannounced at an early gig. Roger's own far noisier 1-2-3-4 punk band had opened for them and Roger dug their style so much he felt compelled to invade the stage and start yapping along.

The guys hit it off so splendidly that the mouthy kid with the ready smile was immediately recruited as the Beat's toaster extraordinary.

The kid, then 18, had been born Roger Charlery in Birmingham, although his folks were from St Lucia, and he was a proper handful. "When I was younger, I used to be a lickle trouble-maker," he confessed. "I used to be a lickle street-fighter. But the only reason I went around hitting people and causing trouble after school with my mates was because there was nothing else to do. Just pure boredom really."

The final recruit was the rather odd figure of their sax player Saxa, who is frequently described as 'ancient' by the rock press despite being merely "around fifty" (he was actually born on 5th January 1930). The boys had spotted him playing in various Handsworth pubs wearing his trademark battered fedora and some rather natty paisley cords. Recognising quality when they saw and heard it, they had offered him a gig right there and then. Just two shows were enough to win the old fella over completely. After the second gig, Saxa told them: "You are my boys, and I want to die playing the saxophone with you. That's where I'm closest to God." But let's pray it ain't soon.

Born Lionel Augustus Martin in Croft Hill, Jamaica, Saxa had played with Prince Buster, Laurel Aitken and Desmond Dekker. He also says that he has blown for the Beatles (or was that Cilla Black?) but I never did stand that up (well you wouldn't, not for Cilla, would you?)

The strangest, or perhaps most visionary thing about the guy is his habit of eating two raw eggs for breakfast, washed down with a heart-starting double brandy. Cheers!

THE first time I saw the Beat live they were supporting The Selecter in Sheffield, and I only caught the sweatier half of the set. But a month later they opened for the Teardrop Explodes and the Human League at the London Lyceum and blew them both clean off stage.

Immediately people started talking about them as "the fourth 2-Tone band", which is probably why they copped so much critical cynicism from jaded music press hacks, but it was obvious to anyone who bothered to listen that these boys weren't aiming for a Ska-based sound.

As I noted at the time, live their music was more like a cross between the Ruts and Big Youth, a merger of more modern musical styles: roots reggae meets new wave attack, pop sensibility and even a pinch of disco.

In November 1979 the 2-Tone label released their debut single as a one-off. Smokey Robinson's 1970 chart-topper 'The Tears Of A Clown' was given the full souped-up Beat treatment, backed with the grittier 'Ranking Full-Stop'. Some Motown purists were unimpressed – it's a song about heartbreak, not an upbeat party number for Chrissakes - but the single did the business. 'Tears' spent eleven weeks on the UK chart, peaking at Number Six. Suddenly record companies were into them like Errol Flynn at a virgins' retreat. But the band held out until they'd negotiated a deal with Arista Records to give them their own Go-Feet label in a business partnership that mirrored the 2-Tone set-up with Chrysalis.

After that they notched up four more Top Ten hits, two Top 30s, a Top 40 and five more that made the lower regions of the charts.

With Britain apparently sewn up, The Beat undertook mammoth tours of Europe, Canada and the USA where they opened for the Pretenders. Playing with Saxa means there's rarely a dull moment. "Our songs tend to evolve as we play them, "explains Dave. "Especially because of Saxa. He reacts very spontaneously and he's likely to take a solo more or less anywhere. We have to style a song around that; you know a solo is coming up, but it might be four bars or it might be 16. It's how the mood takes him. it keeps things fresh. It keeps us on our toes."

DESPITE The Beat's obvious teeny-bop appeal, there has always been a darker side to the band. A cursory look at the lyrics on their debut album, *I Just Can't Stop It*, reveals more controversial subjects

than TV's Question Time. 'Mirror In The Bathroom' concerned Nasty
Nastase style narcissism. 'Click Click' was about suicide, the clicks
being the empty chambers of a gun used in Russian Roulette, while
'Hands Off...She's Mine' far from being the run of the mill tale of
teenage jealousy that feminist critics assumed it to be, was really
about the over-restrictive nature of personal relations - the way some
blokes treat women as their private property.

In August 1980 they decided to make a real stand for the radical
working class politics they supported by releasing a double A-side
single with a punch: 'Best Friend' came with a side order of 'Stand
Down Margaret', and they weren't talking Margaret Rutherford
either. This was aimed straight at the heart of British Prime Minister
Margaret Hilda Thatcher: 'I said, I see no joy / I see only sorry / I see
no chance of your bright new tomorrow / So stand down Margaret /
Stand down please / Stand down Margaret...'

What made the song more interesting / worrying is that as
originally released 'Stand Down Margaret' was only half a song
– specifically it was the second half of a track which was billed as
'Whine & Grine / Stand Down Margaret' on the Beat's debut album.
'Stand Down' actually starts out as a cover of Prince Buster's rude
reggae classic 'Whine & Grine' which famously includes the line

'She wants a rough, rough rider, he want cool, cool stroke...' not an imagine readily associated with the Iron Lady. On the full version, 'Whine & Grine' winds down, and Ranking Roger begins toasting over the same instrumental track, calling for the PM's resignation: 'How can it work if it's all white law?" asks Roger rhetorically. "What a short, sharp lesson, what a third world war...Say too much war in the city yeah/Say too much war in the city, whoa/I sing I said a love and unity, the only way/And unity, the only way/Yeah ya know/You know what!'

As it happens, though, despite being a socialist, Dave Wakeling doesn't even vote. "If voting changed anything they would have made it illegal by now," he says firmly. "I did vote for the Labour government in 1979 because I was afraid the Conservatives would get in and I was terrified by the things they said. So I voted on that one. I didn't think it was going to change anything, and it didn't." As for Thatcher, he says "The only noticeable difference with the Tories in power is that everybody's very demoralized." (Everybody that is, except the merchant bankers, the stockbrokers, the venture capitalists...)

The song has caught on both sides of the pond. Playing America, Roger usually changes the words to 'Stand Down Ronnie' in honour of that nice President Reagan. (Reviewing the album in Sounds however, Pete Silverton later wrote off the 'Margaret' song as facile and claimed that the best bit of politics on the whole platter was... 'Can't Get Used To Losing You' – 'a straight parody of the Andy Williams version, right down to heavy echo on the vocals which capture Williams delivery perfectly.')

The Beat gave all the royalties from the single's sales to the Anti-Nuclear Campaign (more than £15,000 as it happened). Dave Wakeling explained: "We're not frightened or worried, but we must all be prats if we can't do better than blow ourselves up."

Ranking Roger likes to mine the political theme too. "You hear about skinheads going on the rampage or Mods on the beach," he says. "But the only reason they do that is because they've got fuck all else to do. People are frustrated and confused. The only reason I joined the Beat was through boredom. There should be more facilities for kids.

"But you know what we do and say, it all pays off. One time I had this big skinhead come up to me and say, 'I used to be a member of the British Movement but tonight I've seen unity. Fuck them!'"

Some of the dreads weren't soon keen on unity when Roger first made it on to *Top Of The Pops* though.

"I had cussings over working with white boys at first," says Roger, with a grin as wide as the Birmingham Bull Ring. "Some of the dreads would look at me and go 'Cho! How dem white man treat you?' But they're warming to it now.

"Unity though," he says, returning to his theme. That is what it's all about, unity; unity against the Tories, against the fascists and against the people who want to blow the world up.

"If we can create unity then as a band we've achieved something."

It sounds like a cliché, but the Beat are that most rare of commodities – pop stars who care and who can remember what it's like to be the kids in the audience.

PS. The Beat's debut album, *I Just Can't Stop It*, went gold, peaking at Number Three, and stayed on the charts for 32 weeks. (The follow-up, 1981s reggae-influenced *Wha'ppen* (pronounced "War-Pen") also peaked at Number Three but has only managed to attain silver status. The Beat remain a huge live draw however, and a massive force for good. In that sense, they just can't be beat.

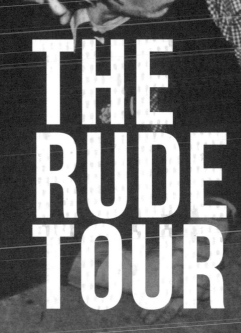

THE
RUDE
TOUR

ON THE RUDE AGAIN: 2-TONE 2

February, 1980

I JOINED THE 2-TONE 2 TOUR FOR A COUPLE OF DELIRIOUS DAYS. THIS IS AN EDITED VERSION OF MY REPORT ON THE EXPERIENCE

ROCK HAD started to get very boring again; very self-important and pompous. Old concepts were rearing up on young shoulders with bands raiding Pink Floyd and Doors back catalogues quite shamelessly in the interests of their Art (capital A of course and nothing to do with such base concepts as pop or rock 'n' roll.)

And the music papers were crammed full of solemn young people, very serious and quite pious, who spoke like dictionaries and wore those dowdy clothes that only the children of the wealthy or the middling wealthy would dream of wearing. It was bleak scenarios all round and a neurotic time had by all.

IAN PAGE of Secret Affair was quite right of course, it was all deadly dull and the time was right for a bona-fide 'New Dance' music. Trouble was despite the excellence of 'Glory Boys' another new dance caught the feet of the nation's youth, one which was a mixture of loads of things but for the sake of simplicity we'll call the 2-Tone sound.

Within months 2-Tone virtually replaced the dying disco rump as the mass dance music of the nation's youth. It was unselfconsciously pop, it was teenage, it was for boys and girls, it had fashions and identity and as a bonus it had a strong morality, a message even, but it didn't come on like Johnny Weissmuller's Tarzan beating its chest about itself which was probably just as well after three years of getting shouted at in the name of cod anarchy.

It all happened quickly and without hype or pretension. First the Specials, then Madness and then the Selecter fired 45 RPM darts at the charts and the nation's heart, with Selecter's debut and the others' follow-ups hitting the Top Ten last November at the same time as the first united 'taking it to the people' 2-Tone tour starring those pioneering Big Three Ska renewal bands.

Sold-out venues, multiple encores, a sense of unity, purpose, even of a crusade, all that and more conspired to give the whole thing legendary status, not least in the eyes of the participants.

A couple of months later and former bottom of the bill openers The Selecter are headlining a 35 date tour of their own, ostensibly to promote their superb debut album Too Much Pressure which even as I type has shot into the Top Ten, at glad-to-be-alive Number Five with a bullet.

And with latest Ska hopefuls, new 2-Tone signings The Bodysnatchers bringing up the rear on the undercard, the impression, especially among punters, that this is the Second 2-Tone Tour is widespread and contagious.

But the 2-Tone collective are wary of trying to re-create the special magic that first outing had engendered. They're also eager to break down any barriers they might inadvertently be building up for themselves - which explains why they have decided to go out on a limb and bring in the rated, but decidedly non-Ska, pop newcomers Holly & The Italians as main tour support. Sadly, albeit predictably, the eye-pleasing Holly's Eyeties have been going down like Leonid Brehznev at a War Widows For Carter Convention but, aw, later for the bloody details...

LEEDS UNIVERSITY is the first gig I catch and the third one on the tour. It's additionally complicated by the fact that the local Student Union are staging a bit of a festival featuring the 2-Tone package in their 2,000-capacity hall with a punkier line-up, with The Gas, The Vibrators and the mighty Ruts in a smaller hall a mere two minutes away down the corridor.

On paper it looked like a dream gig for the modern music lover, with sets synchronised for maximum view-ability; but you don't need me to tell you that in practice it was all about as smooth-running and trouble-free as Ozzy Osbourne addressing a temperance rally. What with miss-timings, cock-ups, and general overcrowding I doubt if many punters managed to see more than one set in its entirety. And the frantic sprints it all entailed coupled with my own total exhaustion (due to having been kept up all the previous night by an insatiable female – age 15 months) means the whole evening survives in my brain merely as a series of hazy impressions...

The Bodysnatchers get everyone dancing (see the Bodysnatchers chapter for full details). But Holly had it much tougher, battling on gamely against audience indifference. Men (and woman) of the match were Selecter who were a frantic blur of energy sounding so proud and strong and confident that all of my criticisms of their Lewisham Odeon debacle became about as relevant to today as Toad The Wet Sprocket are to the New Wave of British Heavy Metal.

Before the Selecter set I wander into the Ruts dressing room with Selecter's dipstick-dimensioned dreadlocked bassist Charley Anderson, both of us attracted by a pleasant but unfamiliar, cough, aroma...

The lads treat us to a preview of their imminent new single, a catchy, gloriously driving Ska-influenced rock sweetmeat entitled 'Staring At The Rude Boys' (not rhubarb, as we originally misheard it) which will be coupled with an impressive lovers rock type affair called 'Love In Vain'.

Chas professes to enjoy the latter greatly, and the conversation gets round to the subject of the Clash's recent excellent reggae dabbling 'Armagidion Time' (shame about the originals). It turns out that Charley had gone to school in Montego Bay with one Michael Campbell, better known as Jamaica's answer to Jimmy Savile, Mikey Dread.

Sad to say, after clocking about five really fiery Ruts numbers I entered into a Maharishi-style meditation which many might have mistaken for a deep sleep. (You can collect your cards as you leave the building – The Editor). Awoken, I mean, disturbed, by Chrysalis pressman Huge Beergut I joined the 2-Tone contingent on the deluxe tour bus where omnipresent bodyguard the ginormous Gunners fan

Steve English was airing the one injury of the night – a nastily sprained ankle caused by a collision with errant skinheads.

"I 'ate skins," moaned the man mountain as he massaged tootsies with more muscles than Eric Fuller's got on his entire puny body, and no-one, but no-one disagreed. Not in public at any rate.

Back at the hotel, those cheeky Bodysnatchers electrify the dying disco (see The Bodysnatchers chapter), leaving the Ruts to fly the flag for rock'n'roll excess. Ladies you have never lived if you haven't suffered, sorry, seen the horrible sight of John 'Segsy' Jennings prancing round naked, and "What is that between his legs, a light switch?" asked a passing Bodysnatcher (unfamiliar with the human male's anatomy for reasons explained elsewhere). Later as a legless Paul 'Foxy' Fox starts pissing in wardrobe and then groping around to find the chain, I decide it's time to hit the sack, as we call Malcolm). Pausing only to order rival scribe Mike Nichols (from Retard Mirror) a wholesome double breakfast for 6.45am, I make my excuses and leave.

NEXT MORNING, well okay, next afternoon, we duck the hung-over Ruts for the relative sanity of the tour bus and the 45 minute drive to Brum. Sprawled over its 'Euro-luxury' interior, among a mass of Dunn & Co trilbies and pork pie hats, are the three bands, a smattering of roadies and such cheerful 2-Tone evergreens as fan-turned-merchandise man Sean, and Selecter 'manager' Juliette Devie, who has gone from Trigger PR to 2-Tone director, and is still as radiant as a 10' be 12' arc lamp (bronchial heave, slap round head etc).

The Selecter are still buzzing about the tour, and the whole idealistic 2-Tonic enterprise: "We see ourselves as one big militant A&R department," says the ever cheerful Charlie. He tells me how on the first 2-Tone tour, Jerry would play them all demos from scores of hopefuls over the coach cassette player, provoking instant considered reviews such as "Shit!", "Bollocks" or "Sign them up."

Pauline stops writing out tonight's set-lists and laughs. "That was the closest we got to a 2-Tone board room," she says.

Compton takes it all very seriously. "Us and the Specials both had the same aims: getting our New Ska sound out there, building up an identity, giving good bands a break." Which sounds more punk than anything most of the established punk bands have achieved if I'm honest.

Some of the 2-Tone takings will be ploughed into a headquarters in Coventry, with some future earnings invested in rehearsal and recording studios.

"It's easy to say something could go wrong somewhere down the

THE FILM OF THE BEST

CHRYSALIS present
BAD MANNERS
THE **bEAT**
THE **BODYSNATCHERS**
MADNESS
THE **SELECTER**
THE **SPECIALS**
in

DANCE CRAZE

PHOTOGRAPHED IN SUPER 35mm Technicolor™   DOLBY STEREO

LIVE ALBUM AVAILABLE ON 2 Recs
MARKETED BY Chrysalis RECORDS

PRODUCED BY GAVRIK LOSEY IN CONJUNCTION WITH TWO TONE FILMS

DISTRIBUTED BY Osiris Films

OF BRITISH SKA... LIVE!

line," Pauline acknowledges. "But the thing is we're experienced, we're aware of the pitfalls." Time alone will tell if her optimism is justified.

Long before then and before the end of this tour I should think seeing as their second single 'Three Minute Hero' appears to have peaked at 16 in the charts, 'Missing Words' will be released as the band's third single. A haunting melodic Davies composition, the general feeling is it has more chance of getting the band back into the Top Ten again.

More importantly it will show that they are capable of varying their sound and retaining their popularity.

Fishing round for clues about the second album proves unproductive. Pauline says that most of them have got new material written but she's keeping the direction close to her formidable chest. Neol just says "it'll be different" while remaining "an extension of what we're doing now." What was that about a riddle wrapped in a mystery inside an enigma?

Pauline simply smiles and says, "Once you decide to take a certain path you're up shit creek without a paddle. We will change, we are changing, but it'll be a natural thing, not forced."

ON THE GENERAL 2-Tone front, there's the Bodysnatchers' fine debut single 'Do Rock Steady' out on March 7, and Specials drummer John Bradbury's own Northern Soul tinged 'Sock It To 'Em, JB' lined up for release before the next Specials disc in May (which a little voice squeaks will probably be 'Rat Race'). And what with the Beat, Bad Manners and Birmingham's psychedelic sounding dub reggae combo UB40 all involved with other labels the only band currently being mooted as the possible next 2-Toners are Coventry's recently-formed Swinging Cats who Neol reckons are "well promising."

But the very success of 2-Tone has inevitably stoked up a reaction; a backlash which has been articulated most strongly I'm sorry to say in Sounds itself by both the revolting Masked Avenger and more seriously by reggae-purist and self-styled Lou Grant type Eric Fuller.

Big El's basic case is: here are these upstart kids and big white Babylon record labels making mountains of moolah from Jamaican artists who won't receive a penny in royalties.

LEAVING ASIDE the facts that 2-Tone are patently not mere Ska-revivalists, that Prince Buster records and lesser Skasters have found fame and sold thousands thanks to 2-Tone, and that contemporary reggae itself is more than 90 per cent based on rip-offs and t'ievery, what is most annoying about the whole accusation is the impression that the whole thing is a calculated exploitation, even though Fuller's own article admits that inefficiency at the Jamaican end is the chief reason for non-compensation.

"What he's talking about is a totally just thing," says Pauline. "Black people have been ripped off since the early Twenties, but the way he's slanting it is just a way to get at 2-Tone. For example, our song 'Everyday' turns out to be really called 'Times Hard' but we didn't change the name to rip anyone off. I only knew the song from discos and that's what I thought it was called, and the copyright people couldn't trace the song with that title...Our end is sorted out now, the rest depends on what the Specials and Madness do."

One thing is for certain; they don't strike me as shysters and once again, expect a riposte from the sorely abused Specials in about two weeks. In the meantime, how about an expose of corruption in the Jamaican reggae biz, El?

At the other end of the spectrum, some hardcore black British reggae musicians are suspicious of the whole 2-Tone schtick and seem to resent its success. Junior Brown is reported to have recently moaned that gigs seemed to be harder to get "now all these white bands are playing reggae."

No matter how much good you do, it seems the higher up the greasy pole you climb the more your arse is a target...

SO controversy, confusion, madness...what else can you possibly want? A gig review? Good thinking. Here we are at Birmingham Top Rank and it's Bodysnatchers time...

There's seven Bodysnatchers. Rhoda (vox), Nicky (bass), Jane (drums), Miranda (sax), Pennie (keyboards), Stella Scunthorpe (rhythm guitar, backing vox), and SJ (lead guitar, backing vox). They're young and inexperienced and they can't play nearly as well as Emerson, Lake & Palmbeach but they're a good deal more enjoyable than any number of the dreaded 'serious musoes'.

Sure there's moments tonight when the ears are offended like during their own 'Happy Time Tune' which slows down every few bars like a record on one of those crank-up gramophones, but in general the 'Snatch, as I like to call them, are a lot more together now than when I last saw them at the Bridgehouse and they weren't bad then.

They're spirited you see, which counts for a lot. Rhoda Dakar is a cracker of a vocalist and a terrifically sassy fronts-personage much prone to dancing, juggling with liver sausages and speaking her mind. When some drunken Brummie wag shouts "Show us yer minge," she turns on him and cut him down to about half an inch high with an ace selection of abuse which wouldn't have sounded out of place on the Shed terraces.

With her long dancing legs, Sixties mini and beehive hair she sums up the 'Snatch sound in much the same way as Chas Smash personifies Madness.

The set is replete with familiar songs from my early teens such as '007 (Shanty Town)', 'Monkey Spanner' and 'Double Barrel'. In general, their sound is more in the vein of such originals than say Selecter who use the old as a base to build something new and very much their own from. The only exception is 'The Boiler', the band's emotive tale of a rape attack which although heartfelt and harrowing sticks out in a set of general good cheer like a laughing clown at a dead child's wake.

The other originals are fun and games type affairs in the style of their vintage Trojan predecessors, and the imminent b-side 'Ruder Than You' – a testament to the spunk of rude girls - in particular illustrates that they're capable of cutting it on their own terms: 'Now rude boys don't have it their own way / Hey listen we have something to say! / We're Rude girls - you better watch out / Rude girls...now there's more of us about Rude girls...'

Along with the rest of the Brum audience I clap and cheer until they encore but was this only to get another glimpse of SJ, a woman so moodily beautiful that I couldn't believe Playboy talent scouts aren't camped out in front of the stage, with their Bolex in hand (That's quite enough of that – Rock Against Sexism).

While I smile along with the 'Snatch I almost cry tears of frustration for poor old Holly & The Italians (the band are so-called because two of them are Yanks and one of them is English.) They're one of the more promising girl-fronted 'New Wave pop bands' (God, doncha just hate smartarse pigeonholes) flourishing in the wake of Chrissie Hynde. Trouble is they ain't Ska, and while most of the crowd stare at them apathetically, the bigoted birdbrains down at the front start up a set-long chant of "Fuck off!"

Jeez! 'Tell That Girl To Shut Up' is a classic song, but the band aren't fashionable and that's enough to set off the morons.

After the Eyeties' brave promising set, the DJ plays PIL's

'Public Image' and the audience who had just booed a good band off stage for being different sing along with all the words parrot fashion, apparently not realising that Lydon's lyrics are a plea for individuality... There's more chance of finding a *Dr Who* alien here than a sense of irony. And there we are back with the Bodysnatchers...

It makes you feel like jacking it all in. But not for long though because before long the Selecter are making like the Magnificent Seven again and gunning down all possible doubts about the point of it all, and their own excellence.

IT'S THE BIG Bounce dance stance, the big guns of Coventry shooting out pop shots non-stop with the beautiful, vivacious Pauline fronting a whirlpool of visual action that don't stop once for the duration. Watching the band is like watching a hornet's nest after you've thrown rocks at it. They're up and down, in and out, jiving and dancing all over the shop. Even Desmond deserts his keyboards every now and again to streak up front. But unlike hornets they're a highly individual looking bunch.

There's Pauline of course in her trilby and Red Nose tunic; Neol looking like an animated Walter Jabsco, Crompton Young and fresh-faced Charley with that Leo the Lion mane, and Gappa who's so stern he burns you up with his eyes.

My niggling reservation about the album was that Gappa's vocals were underplayed a bit. But that certainly ain't true live where he's equal partner with Pauline leading the band through the classics. The great singles. 'On My Radio' with its huff and puff bruff anger and Sparksian chorus, 'Three Minute Hero' your workday dream, 'Missing Words' which is sooo catchy. And then 'The Selecter' itself with Gaps doing some classic reggae growling, Pauline and Desmond's 'They Make Me Mad' with those proud assertive lyrics, such a welcome antidote to the standard Rasta attitude to women...

Slowly the pressure builds up through the high quality originals and the superb rearrangements of old classics, building up the tension, then Desmond's organ goes and he loses his cool and kicks it over, storming off stage...all just before 'Too Much Pressure' and he's so fuming, so angry, that once again I'm fooled by the fight scene 'cos it looks so real and how the hell do I know he ain't using it as an excuse to beat shit out of his fellows?

Both he and Gappa dive into the crowd who've already been

repelled from the stage once. And the roadies and Big Steve English struggle to rescue them from the eager sweaty throng in time to pull them off stage at the end of the song which is bridged into a version of the Upsetters' 'Live Injection'.

The encore is 'James Bond' and the absence of the organ and the fact that the band are about to tear into each other in frustration backstage does nothing to detract from the joy of the oblivious crowd. As Pauline and the gang trot off there's another crowd stage invasion. A white rudie grabs the mike and starts up a chant of 'Rude Boys!'. Spontaneously he reaches out to black kid. They put their arms round each other's shoulders and give the crowd the thumbs up signs.

That, my friends is 2-Tone in a nutty shell.

THE SPECIALS

THE BODYSNATCHERS
+ GO-GO'S
ON CERTAIN GIGS ONLY

JUNE 4*
GT YARMOUTH, Tiffanys

JUNE 5*
SKEGNESS, Sands Show Bar

JUNE 6*
BRIDLINGTON, Royal Spa Pavilion

JUNE 8*
LEEDS, University

JUNE 9
BARROW-IN-FURNESS, Civic Hall

JUNE 10
BLACKPOOL, Tiffanys

JUNE 11
COLWYN BAY, Pier Pavilion

JUNE 12
FRIARS AYLESBURY

JUNE 13
WORTHING, Assembly Rooms

JUNE 15
BOURNEMOUTH, Stateside

JUNE 16*
HASTINGS, Pier Pavilion

JUNE 17*
MARGATE, Winter Gardens

JUNE 18*
SOUTHEND, Cliffs Pavilion

JUNE 19*
PORTSMOUTH, Guild Hall

BRAVO DELTA '80...

SEASIDE SPECIALS TOUR...

...IS IN TOWN... OVER!

RUDE GIRL

RUDER
THAN
YOU

RUDER THAN YOU

SKINHEAD MOONSTOMP, SYMARIP

SKA and Trojan Reggae provided the joyous musical soundtrack for the hard-living, fun-loving, two-fisted English working-class youth cult phenomenon of the Sixties, Skinhead. But who were the skinheads, and where did they come from?

Skins evolved out of a Spartan branch of mod called the Suits who were first spotted on the London club scene around 1965, at a time when Mod culture was becoming increasingly commercialised, and its sartorial values were fraying at the edges. The Suits were very much a dapper, down to earth alternative to the dubious lure of psychedelic music, and the coming Hippie movement. Dull drugs, pacifism, flower power scruffiness and musical self-indulgence had little appeal to everyday hooligan youth. Imported West Indian culture was different, however, and its music, fashions and attitudes were to exert a major influence on the evolution of the distinctive skinhead style.

Ska arrived in Britain in the early Sixties via West Indian immigrants and was accepted as a credible alternative to American soul on the hard-mod scene. In Britain it got called 'blue-beat' because most of this exciting new music was being released on Melodisc's Bluebeat label. Groups such as Laurel Aitken & the Carib Beats, Basil Gabbidon's Mellow Larks and Desmond Dekker and the Aces (see Pioneers) were at the forefront. The first British blue-beat hit was Millie Small's bouncy bundle of joy 'My Boy Lollipop' (which contrary to urban myth did not feature Rod 'the Mod' Stewart on mouth organ, but bluesman Pete Hogman; it did have the great Ernest Ranglin, later of the Wailers, on guitar though).

THE SKA REVIVAL

Ska was the music of the first-generation British black kids and those teenage immigrants who also adopted their own look and a name - the Rude Boys. This was the identity assumed by Jamaica's tough and volatile young ghetto yobs, kids who were known for their bloody gang wars and general lawlessness. Ska lyrics were often aimed at persuading the Rudies to cool it, but perversely the Wailers' first single 'Simmer Down' and later songs such as 'Rude Boy' and 'Jail House' only helped to glorify the cult.

The Rude Boy rig-out that was sported by West Indian youths in South London was a direct ancestor of skinhead style: 'crombie-type coats, trousers worn higher than the norm to emphasise white socks and black shoes, all topped off with pork pie hats and wrap-around shades. Throw in English braces, army or work boots, donkey jackets, sheepskins, scarves and cravats and that's pretty much early skin style in a nutshell.

Razor hair-partings also originated with the young blacks, and it's highly likely that the skinhead crop, although having roots in the mod crew-cut, was accentuated as a means of imitating the Rude Boys' hair style.

In the beginning these surly shaven-headed white kids, first seen in South London, were known by a variety of names (peanuts, cropheads, boiled eggs, no-heads and so on) but they had become identified as Skinheads by as early as 1967. In Jamie Mandelkau's *Buttons: The Making Of a President*, the biography of the Islington-born British Hell's angel leader Peter 'Buttons' Welsh, he talks of battling "the Walthamstow Skinheads" at the tail end of that year. Of all the names, only skinhead really did justice to the new cult's hard, aggressive and uncompromisingly working-class stance.

By the summer of '68, skinheads had taken off nationwide as the working class youth look, spawning a new media demon: the boot-boy. Ian Walker writing in *New Society* claimed to have seen 4,000 skinheads running rampage at one soccer match. 'They all wore bleached Levis, Dr Martens, a short scarf tied cravat style, cropped hair,' he wrote, adding: 'They looked like an army and after the game went into action like one'. By the following summer the cult had reached its peak, and Skinhead was 'the look' for young working class kids. Fighting, dancing, football, fashion – these were the skins' main preoccupations. Violence was largely territorial and occurred mostly at or around football grounds, although the mass media was more interested in the shock-horror mileage to be had from stories of skinhead attacks on minorities – homosexuals, squaddies, long-hairs (from my own childhood I can recall 'hippy-types' getting off at the next stop on the train rather than risk a beating from the kids off the Ferrier Estate in South East London) and Pakistanis, although these attacks were more to do with cultural than racial differences. A fine distinction to be made after you'd just been clobbered over the head with a half-brick to be sure, but an important one nonetheless. The young Pakistani immigrants were different, unlike the West Indian kids they didn't mix, and they weren't cool. They were equally disliked by the West Indian skinheads, or Afro Boys as they became known.

A Rudie spin-off, the Afro Boys were plentiful in cities like London and Birmingham, and were equals in skinhead gangs, initially at least; although the skinhead kids interviewed in The Paint House testify that tensions stirred up by sexual rivalry generated ill-feeling. Battling at football matches – which neither began nor ended with skinheads – resulted in the adoption of various weapons or 'tools', possibly the nastiest being home-made Kung Fu metal filed into star shapes to be chucked like darts (which were also popular) at your opponents. Millwall fans came up with the 'Millwall brick', a cosh made from a simple tabloid newspaper folded until it became lethally hard. The most popular 'helpers' however, were the simple metal comb and steel-capped Dr Marten work boots. It's unlikely that the good nineteenth century Bavarian, Doctor Marten, had the slightest idea of just how seminal his patented Air-Wair soles (resistant to fat, acid, oil, petrol, and alkali, and topped off handsome leather uppers) were to become for generations of hardcore British hooligans. Martens, or DMs, were an essential ingredient of the early skinhead look. Then they were usually brown or cherry red, and just eight hole affairs as a rule. Girls never wore DMs, they favoured monkey boots.

The very best guide to the evolution of skinhead sartorial style over the golden age of '68 to '71 was written by Jim Ferguson and published in Nick Knight's Skinhead book (although his essay and Harry Hawke's handsome reggae discography are the only things worth buying the book for, as the rest consists of over-generalised, under-researched, pseudo-sociological cobblers about the late Seventies skinhead resurgence). Simplifying, early workday/football wear would be boots, braces (to emphasis working class origins and loyalties), any unfashionable shirt, an army or RAF great coat, a Levi or Wrangler jacket, or a donkey jacket. For best, dances and such like, all skins aspired to possess a decent suit, preferably a mohair, 2-Tone or Prince of Wales check affair, worn with brogues, and later loafers. The all-time favourite skinhead coat was the sheepskin overcoat – 'crombies didn't really catch on properly until suede-head time. Hair was razor cropped, but heads were never shaved bald. The razors were set to different lengths, 1-5, with the number one crop being the shortest. The favourite shirt was the Ben Sherman with button-down collars and back-pleats. Bens were usually checked (never white) and worn with the top button undone and the sleeves turned up once. Brutus check shirts and later the humble Fred Perry were also acceptable. Smarter skins replaced Levi red-tag jeans with Sta-Prest trousers.

Black and white skins mixed freely at dance-halls. Reggae was 'the' skinhead music, but it was a markedly different reggae from the simple Ska the rudies had introduced Mods to earlier on in the decade. Around 1966, Ska in Jamaica had developed into Rock Steady, just as US R&B developed into Soul. Alton Ellis' definitive dance hit 'Rock Steady' was typical of the new genre which itself developed, until by 1969 it was producing massive British chart hits like Desmond Dekker's 'Israelites'. This 'reggae of the '69 kind' was a major chart factor for the following few years with some Jamaican artists quite shamelessly pandering to their English audience (the best example of overtly skinhead-orientated reggae was the Symarips' 'Skinhead Moonstop').

In the earlier part of the decade a blue-beat aficionado would have to go to Brixton (where Somerleyton Road rather than Railton Road was then the front-line), in Lambeth; and clubs like the Ram Jam in Brixton Road to hear the music, or South East London pubs like the Three Tuns. We would trek to Lewisham market where the latest imports were stocked. But as the music moved into pop's mainstream, so reggae nights became regular features of dance halls like the local Palais.

US soul was still extremely popular too, and artists like Booker T had a large skinhead following, although inevitably the music lived more through DJs in the pubs and clubs than on stage.

No youth cult stands still however. The skinhead look became progressively smarter, with boots and braces dropped in favour of belts and loafers even during the day, evolving into the suede-head style. Suede-heads wore their hair longer – it was comb-able – and favoured the 'crombie coat (an Abercrombie overcoat, preferably with a velvet collar). Some suedes developed a 'city gent' look sporting bowlers and brollies, although the classic suede image was the Harrington jacket – named after Rodney Harrington who wore it in the TV show *Peyton Place* (like the city gent look, it was originally briefly fashionable with Mods) – Sta-Prest trousers (white ones looked best) and ox-blood Royals. By the end of '71, suede-head had developed into the 'smoothie' look with the hair even longer, Fair Isle yoke pullovers, polo necks and later tank tops, and shirts with hideous rounded collars. The favoured smoothie shoes were called Norwegians. They were lace-ups and had a basket weave design on the front. With the gargantuan growth of glam and glitter between '71 and '73, Skinhead was finished as a mass movement, although some die-hards dyed their Docs rather than ditch them.

Now it was the turn of ex-Mods like Bowie and Bolan, and bands like Slade and Sweet to influence the teeny hordes. Their gift to the nation was a generation of kids sporting gaudy clothes, sparkle in their hair, and ludicrous platform boots…it was a style nightmare. Glam was more a fashion than a cult, led by bands that specialised in superb camp pop corn. For the original skins it seemed that the world had turned upside down.

But as I write about at length in my book Hoolies, skinhead didn't entirely die. Kept alive by scattered individuals, from 1976 it began to grow as a cult again, incubating on the new punk scene. Before 2-Tone, the main musical draw for the resurgent skins were hard prototype Oi bands such as Sham 69 and Menace, who were very aggressive and determinedly populist; although original Trojan reggae was still very much part of the skinhead equation.

For the first time, politics mired the scene with both far left and far right battling for the hearts and minds of the young hooligans. As we have seen elsewhere in this book, politically motivated violence caused problems for 2-Tone at the start, particularly for Madness and The Selecter. At a Bad Manners show at London's Electric Ballroom in 1980, a neo-Nazi leapt on stage and tried to stab Buster Bloodvessel; mercifully Louis Alphonso clouted the creep around the head with his guitar.

An absolutely crazy development; to be a racist skin made as much sense as being a Jewish anti-Semite. But equally crazy was the assumption made by the middle-class media that all skins were Nazis.

The Rude Boy (and Rude Girl) cult which grew up around 2-Tone was a smart, healthy reminder that skinhead culture had its roots in black music.

Their arrival can be traced directly to 2-Tone's smartly suited Rude Boy logo man, known to his fans as Walter Jabsco. Walt was Jerry's big idea, and the Specials bassist Horace Panter had drawn him, based on an old Peter Tosh LP cover. Jabsco had the archetypal Rude look: a smart black suit, white shirt, skinny black tie, white socks, black loafers and a tasty titfer. The only real person who carried off the image better was Specials roadie Cardboard (Steve Eaton), who was a Coventry style icon, and who ended up as the debonair cover boy for the Selecter's 'Too Much Pressure' album.

Rude Boys and Rude Girls were directly inspired into being by the bands they followed. In London, they were drawn originally from the ranks of the capital's Mod and Skinhead scenes. There was a distinct rude look, identical for both sexes. Levi Sta-Prest strides, or 2-Tone mohair ones. Braces, button-down shirts, loafers, white or red socks. Harrington jackets, pork pie hats or Trilbies.

Boys' hair was shorter, cropped of course, but closer to the Mod's French crew cut than the skin's number one. But as the music became more mainstream and the fans got younger so the look became more sexually distinct - boys going for the full-on Walt Jabsco black two-piece suits, girls opting for dresses with black and white geometric patterns, black shoes (brogues or loafers), white tights and large ear-rings. The rude teen look went deeper and lasted longer in the Midlands than it did in London where it swiftly submerged into Skinhead with 2-Tone having the effect of reviving the skin style which had started to decline after Sham. 2-Tone and Rude style also had the distinction of being the first youth cult to attract significant numbers of black and mixed-race youth since Skinhead a decade before, and many more of them too. It was also the first British youth cult to appeal to many thousands of young Asian teenagers.

As US band The Toasters would later write: 'You don't need no member to let yourself in/You don't need no language or colour of skin/Don't need no money to make a contribution/To be a part of the 2-Tone revolution....' (The Toasters, '2-Tone Army').

Rude style also had far more in common with the sartorial values of Sixties skins than the scruffy bald punks that had pirated their name.

Of course, there was one big difference between the first wave of skinheads and their successors. Back in the sixties the style evolved naturally. In the later revivals, kids were consciously retro. They were adopting a uniform that was frozen in time rather than going with the flow of a developing youth cult. By 1981, you could argue that the true inheritors of the hard-mod ethos, and that of the original skinheads, were dressing Casual.

167

THE
PIONEERS

TRAIN TO SKAVILLE: THE PIONEERS

Ska, from which skinhead reggae blossomed, was a Jamaican development of American R&B embellished with jazz touches like the omnipresent horn section. Wailers guitarist Ernest Ranglin said that the word Ska was cooked up to describe the 'Skat! Skat! Skat!' scratching guitar strum that goes behind. Emerging as a recognised form in 1956, by 1963 Ska dominated the Jamaican music scene and also reflected the optimism of the people who's just been granted Independence under a Jamaican Labour party government.

No study of 2-Tone could be complete with at least tipping our metaphorical titfer to the musicians who pioneered the sounds of Ska and the uplifting Skinhead Reggae that followed it. Many could be mentioned, but here are my own Big Five:

PRINCE BUSTER

'Come over, get me brush up/Going to rub a pussy here tonight/
Heavy rain falling/I can feel my [horn burst] getting stiff in hand/
Spunky, spunky night in Big Five/Spunky, spunky night in Big Five...'

The Prince, the star who "sold the heat with a rocksteady beat", was
born plain old Cecil Bustamente Campbell in Kingston, Jamaica, on
28th May 1938. Although allegedly controversial in respect of some
of his business dealings (e.g. the paying of musicians), the records he
recorded for the Blue Beat label made former amateur boxer Buster
one of the most influential and important figures in Ska history.

Campbell started singing in nightclubs when he was eighteen, but
his talent wasn't recognised until after mobile sound system parties
had become the rage in JA, and even then it wasn't for his voice. He
was hired initially as a minder! But in 1960 he released 'Oh Carolina',
with its African inspired drumming, and scored an instant hit. His
subsequent Blue Beat recordings were a major influence on the
growth of Ska as a distinct musical form.

Buster toured the UK, appearing on TV pop show Ready Steady
Go in 1964. His biggest UK hit was 'Al Capone' which reached No
18 in 1967. His rude reggae song 'Big Five' (based on 'Rainy Night
In Georgia'!) was banned, and of course partly inspired the career of
Judge Dread.

Prince Buster converted to Islam after meeting world
heavyweight boxing champ Muhammad Ali in England, and
adopted the name Muhammed Yusef Ali.

DESMOND DEKKER

'I want you to know who's the King of Ska/The King of Ska' is right
here on top.'

Desmond Dekker was the first Jamaican reggae star to achieve
genuine international success. His haunting 1969 smash hit
'Israelites', a UK chart-topper for Dekker and his backing band
the Aces, made him the ace face of skinhead reggae. He had more
singles success than Bob Marley had done in his lifetime. The
Desmond who had a barrow in the market place in the Beatles'
'O-Bla-Di O-Bla-Da' was Paul McCartney's nod to Dekker.

Born Desmond Adolphis Dacres in St Andrew, Jamaica, on 16th
July 1941, Dekker was an orphan who started his working life

as a welder. In early 1961, aged 19, he passed an audition with the Beverley's record label and proceeded to notch up a string of homeland hits, including 'King Of Ska', before he rather cynically reinvented himself as a Rude Boy in 1967 - Desmond was the kindest-hearted 'delinquent' you could ever meet; he was a gentle, soulful guy with a spiritual streak. But the rebranding helped him make it big time. Songs such as that year's '007 (Shanty Town)', which was his first UK chart hit, and 'Tougher Than Tough' built his profile. Many of the first British punks would cite him as an influence.

Dekker moved to England after the success of 'Israelites' but sadly, despite later signing to Stiff, the hits ran out for him after 1975, and in 1984 he went bankrupt.

Desmond Dekker died on 25th May 2006, after suffering a heart attack at his home in Surrey. He was 64, and due to start a European tour the following week.

LAUREL AITKEN

'Everybody knows I'm a rude boy / Walking the streets of dreams...'

Original rude boy Lorenzo Aitken is rightly regarded as the "Godfather of Ska." Born in Cuba on 22 April 1927, his family emigrated to Kingston, Jamaica, when Laurel was eleven. The star, who was later dubbed the Boss Skinhead, worked for the Jamaican Tourist Board singing mento songs to holiday-makers before becoming a local nightclub singer. Before Ska, Aitken's recordings were mento – a pre-reggae Jamaican folk music similar to calypso - and rock 'n' roll. His 1958 single 'Little Sheila' (produced by Chris Blackwell, who was to form Island Records) was the first Jamaican single released in the UK.

Laurel moved to Brixton in 1960 and released fifteen singles for Blue Beat in three years. But it would be his classic recordings for Pama Records such as 'Landlord & Tenants' and 'Fire In Mi Wire' that cemented his role in the development of Ska. Although Judge Dread was always more moved by 1969's 'Pussy Price Gone Up.'

Aitken finally hit the UK charts with 'Rudi Got Married' in 1980, on the back of the 2-Tone explosion that he and the other pioneers had made happen. After his death in 2005, a blue plaque was erected at his Leicester home, thanks in part, to the tireless campaigning of Symarips bassist, and Ska fanatic Mark Wyeth, QC

JIMMY CLIFF

'Yeah, the harder they come, the harder they'll fall one and all/
What I say now, what I say now, awww'

Jimmy Cliff is the great survivor of Jamaican music. Born James
Chambers in St James, on April 1st 1948, Jimmy's career began in
Ska and ended with a spectacular career rebirth this year (2011)
as he recorded with long-time fan Tim Armstrong from Rancid.
Last year he was admitted to the Rock'n' Roll Hall of Fame and is
the only living musician to hold a Jamaican Order Of Merit – the
highest honour granted by the Jamaican government.

Cliff began writing songs while he was at primary school in
St. James, and as a secondary schoolboy in Kingston he entered
talent shows and talked himself into his first recording deal. He
was 14 when he had his first Jamaican hit with 'Hurricane Hattie'.
He later signed to Island and moved to England where he would
have two Top Ten hits – 1969's 'Wonderful World, Beautiful
People' and 1970's 'Wild World' – a cover of a Cat Stevens
number. His self-penned anti-war anthem peaked at No 48, but
Bob Dylan called it "The best protest song I have ever heard."

'Don't be alarmed', she told me the telegram said/But mistress
Brown your son is dead'/And it came from Vietnam, Vietnam,
Vietnam, Vietnam/Vietnam, Vietnam - hey – Vietnam/Somebody
please stop that war now!'

Jimmy Cliff appeared in the boss reggae movie The Harder
They Come – the soundtrack featured his moving 'Many Rivers
To Cross.' His last UK hit came with 1994's cover of Johnny
Nash's 'I Can See Clearly Now', which was played in the film
Cool Runnings.

In November 2011 Jimmy released his 'Sacred Fire' EP
produced by Tim Armstrong. It included covers of 'Ruby Soho'
by Rancid, Dylan's 'A Hard Rain's Gonna Fall' and two versions
of the Clash's 'The Guns of Brixton', plus two Cliff originals.

MILLIE SMALL

'My boy Lollipop/You make my heart go giddy-up/You are as
sweet as candy/You're my sugar dandy...'

Not the biggest star in the reggae world, in any sense, but
Millie (born Millicent Dolly May Small, on 6th October 1946)

deserves a place in The Top Five for being Ska's first international star. Her infectious 1964 smash 'My Boy Lollipop' – a cover of a 1950s r&b song by Dionne Bromfield – was a hit in the USA, Eire, Scandinavia and Australia as well as here where it reached the No 2 slot and spent 18 weeks in the charts. (The follow-up, 'Sweet William', peaked at No.30).

Jamaican Millie, the daughter of a sugar plantation owner, was the first artist to have a hit in the Ska style. She was billed as "The Blue Beat Girl" on the US release. And she was only 17 at the time.

EPILOGUE

EPILOGUE

The sun appeared to have set on 2-Tone in 1986 when Madness and Bad Manners – the last bands skanking – both called it a day. Obituaries appeared in the music press, and the corpse was interred in a natty black and white shroud.

Yet here we are 33 years later and pretty much every Ska band you have ever heard of is back and touring, some for shedloads more money than they ever got back in the Eighties. Some are even writing new material.

As I write Madness have just headlined Kenwood House as Madness XL with an orchestra. The reformed although sadly depleted Specials have become festival favourites. The tireless Selecter's 40th anniversary tour is spanning nine countries, including the USA and Germany; and Bad Manners seem to gig endlessly.

On the downside we recently lost Ranking Roger.

There are spin-off bands, side projects, and marvellous new Ska groups blossoming all around the globe. While in Coventry, a whole 2-Tone village sprang up in the Stoke area of the city, including a museum, a restaurant, a cafe, a venue, the 2-Tone Trail and a Walk Of Stars – all the incredible achievement of Ska fan Pete Chambers, supported at every turn by all of our skanking favourites.

Why did he happen? Because he says his mate got approached by two Japanese tourists in Coventry city centre who were looking for "the 2-Tone museum". His friend had to tell them no such museum existed. At the time, there was nothing to suggest the glorious musical phenomenon had even originated in Coventry. Pete was so disgusted that he created the 2-Tone trail, covering different locations around the city that were pertinent to 2-Tone. "Funnily enough a lot of the venues sold alcohol," he says. "But that's probably the same with any music genre..." He wrote a booklet and sold badges at the tourist office. He says: "That inspired me and of course was it was never going to be enough. I went to the local museum, The Herbert, and staged a temporary museum – a precursor to what we have now. They couldn't keep it permanently, which was a good thing in a way as it spurred us on to create our museum. We eventually had a stall in the market that was all about 2-Tone for the 30th anniversary in 2009." They then moved it into Coventry University and finally began the village proper. That was up and running by the time the first edition of this book was published in 2011.

But 2-Tone lives on outside of the Cathedral city too of course. Dance floors still get delirious to blue-beat everywhere from Mexico to the Medway towns. You hear it at scooter rallies, on TV adverts and on jingles; and Ska bands flourish in Tokyo and Tijuana, Boston and Beijing, and all points in between.

The universal appeal of music based on the joyous Jamaican beat of the Sixties is hard to avoid. It's the sound that refused to die! Here's what happened to the English bands who revived it.

THE SPECIALS

The Specials debut album sold in excess of one million copies worldwide. Their biggest hit 'Ghost Town' shifted more than 600,000 copies in 1981 in the UK alone. Yet, this wasn't enough to prevent Neville Staple, Lynval Golding and Terry Hall leaving the band shortly after it topped the charts to form the Fun Boy Three. Why? There were moans about Jerry's controlling nature, but largely they'd had enough of the politics around the scene; the riots, the rucks and the racists. And Terry Hall had the hump because he felt his songwriting didn't get the credit it deserved.

The Fun Boy Three were an immediate smash, notching up seven hits including 'The Lunatics Have Taken Over The Asylum', 'It Ain't What You Do It's The Way That You Do It' (which launched Bananarama) and 'Really Saying Something'. But they disbanded in 1983, with Terry leaving to form Colour Field, who managed just one Top 20 hit in '85.

Jerry responded to their defection by bringing in new vocalists Rhoda Dakar from The Bodysnatchers and Stan Campbell who would sing the band's biggest post-split hit, the rousing protest song 'Free Nelson Mandela' but would quit immediately after the recording.

Jerry changed the group's name back to The Special AKA. Their first single release, a revamp of Rhoda's date rape lament 'The Boiler', was largely untroubled by radio plays and peaked at 35. The next single, the preachy 'Racist Friend' bombed. It took 'Mandela' to take them back into the Top Ten, but after that the hits dried up. The Specials had had two gold albums, but their expensive third full-length release, 'In The Studio' failed even to go silver.

Gutted, Dammers broke up the band to concentrate on political activism, especially Artists Against Apartheid.

After the Fun Boy Three, Neville Staple formed Special Beat in 1990 with The Beat's Ranking Roger. They played both band's hits live. As the US Ska exploded, Nev moved to the West Coast where he collaborated with brilliants bands such as No Doubt, Rancid, Unwritten Law, and Canada's The Planet Smashers. By 2004, he was back in the UK performing with his own Neville Staple Band playing Specials hits and Ska classics to appreciative audiences – including a Benny Hill Statue appeal variety show in Essex, where the eccentric bill included Brian Conley, Rick Wakeman, Grandad Jim from EastEnders, Right Said Fred and the Cockney Rejects.

All of the other Specials stars were involved in musical projects, many of them very good indeed. Lynval Golding played and recorded with Pama International (and also Seattle's Stiff Upper Lips.). After the split, Roddy Radiation led new rockabilly band the Tearjerkers, then joined The Specials 2, and Pauline Black's Three Men And Black before settling down with Coventry-based Ska and rockabilly fusion band The Skabilly Rebels. The late John Bradbury went to work with JB's All-Stars (sometimes a 16-piece) who were eventually dropped by RCA for failing to deliver hits. Horace Panter joined General Public with Dave Wakeling and Ranking Roger; he then played with various bands including Box Of Blues, The Specials 2, The Tones and the Coventry Ska-Jazz Orchestra....

Most of these projects had musical merit, but none of them were commercially successful compared to The Specials. So it wasn't too surprising when in March 2008, Terry Hall revealed that the band were reforming. On 6 September 2008, six members of the former Specials performed on the Main Stage at Bestival, billed as the 'Surprise Act'. A full 30th anniversary tour followed in 2009, and the Specials have been playing ever since.

Initially only Jerry Dammers wasn't involved. He described the reunion as a "takeover" and claimed he had been forced out of the band. In reality it was a clash of ambition. Jerry went along for a couple of rehearsals, but he wasn't invited back. "I wanted to move the old songs on a bit, add something modern to them," he told the Guardian. "They weren't interested at all."

He'd argued that they should record new material and push some barriers. The others wanted a retro tour, a tribute to their past, playing all the old hits. "Nostalgia was considered a mental illness in the Victorian era, a morbid obsession with the past," Jerry joked.

With neither side prepared to bend, Dammers pushed on with his Spatial AKA Orchestra, a sprawling 18-strong line-up that takes much of its creative impulse from cosmic jazz big band master Sun Ra and his Arkestra, along with many things psychedelic and the odd pinch of Dada

It's certainly different: a collision of ska, afro rhythms, futurism and free jazz that says "We're not in the Coventry of 1979 anymore." Where they are though is open to debate. Possibly Mars. They do Sun Ra numbers, they do Alice Coltrane. They even do the Batman theme... They're kitsch, kaleidoscopic and crackers, they wear Ancient Egyptian masks and robes...and they've been doing it in various forms since 2006.

The reformed Specials still play to this day but now there are only three of them: Terry, Lynval and Horace.

Drummer John "Brad" Bradbury died in December 2015 aged 62, just three months after the death of Cuban born Ska legend Rico Rodriguez MBE. He was 80.

Neville Staple quit in the Spring of 2013, citing fractured relationships inside the band, and revealing that guitarist Roddy Radiation was so pissed off he had "considered suicide". Roddy, birth name Byers, left in February 2014 to concentrate his energy on his Skabilly Rebels outfit. He appeared as special guest on Dave Wakeling's English Beat UK tour. He later teamed up with Neville and performed on Rude Rebels, the album Nev made with his wife Christine "Sugary" Staple. Neville Staple also released the albums *Ska Crazy* (2014) and *Return Of Judge Roughneck* (2018). The Staples also set up the Skamouth festival and Nev and his Neville Staple Band have supported the Musicians Against Homelessness movement.

Tragedy struck when Neville's grandson Fidel Glasgow, 21, was fatally stabbed in Coventry last September. Nev and Sugary responded by collaborating with reggae legend Dandy Livingstone (who wrote Rudy, 'A Message To You') to release new single 'Put Away Your Knifes' as an appeal to young people involved in knife crime. Neville said, "We are dedicating the song to my grandson Fidel and to everyone else out there, who has been affected by violent crimes. It's time we take back some control and teach the youth right from wrong, and the consequences of their actions. This song is highlighting the pain and the anger being inflicted on the families too. It asks the youths to just stop, think and put down the knives! Even while we were in the studio recording this, my wife Sugary and I became very emotional. It hurts bad when you lose someone so young in the family, but it's even harder when you know that someone took their life early."

Neville and Sugary also used the song to highlight the terrific work

of Victim Support too, promoting their services to encourage more support and donations, especially for what Victim Support do for families affected by knife crime.

Footnote: About 15 years ago, Horace, Lynval and Nev went into a studio with Jerry to record 'Victims Of War', a song Dammers had written after the beginning of the Iraq War. The song, which Jerry describes as being "where Ghost Town left off" has never been released.

MADNESS

The writing was on the wall for Madness in October 1982 when Mike' Barso' Barson told them he was leaving the band the following year. Monsieur Barso had written and arranged their most memorable songs, as well as 1985s *Mad Not Mad* album (released on their own Zarjazz label) which was disappointing in both sales and musical quality. Two of the singles from the album failed, for the first time, to make the Top 20. The one hit, 'Yesterday's Men' peaked at 18 and the title began to feel like a prophecy.

The lads worked on a follow-up album, but "musical differences" raised their head and in September 1986 the band announced they were calling it a day. Mike Barson came back for the farewell single, '(Waiting For) The Ghost Train', which again peaked at 18. Two years later, Suggs, Chas Smash, Lee Thompson and Chrissy Boy attempted to come back as The Madness, but after one album and two flop singles they packed it in.

Late in 1991, Stiff re-released 'It Must Be Love' which went Top Ten the following February; a subsequent singles compilation *Divine Madness* topped the charts. Madness announced a comeback, with the original line-up. Two 'Madstock' open-air concerts at Finsbury Park that August were sell-outs, attracting more than 75,000 nutty fans whose boisterous dancing led to reports of a North London earthquake (seriously). A live album made the Top 30, although the single, a cover of Jimmy Cliff's 'The Harder They Come' peaked at No.44. Christmas tours and three more Madstock festivals followed throughout the Nineties. And in 1999, 'Lovestruck', taken from their album *Wonderful*, found them back in the Top Ten.

A Madness musical, *Our House*, ran in the West End at the Cambridge Theatre from October 2002 until August 2003; and has since toured the UK.

The lads formed The Dangermen as a side project in the Noughties, but Chrissie Boy quit in 2005, replaced for live shows by Kevin Burdette.

Their album, *The Dangermen Sessions Volume 1* (V2 Records) did okay, but the singles bombed. By Christmas 2006, Chrissie Boy was back. They scored minor hits the following year with 'Sorry' and 'NW5'.

In 2008, they unveiled huge chunks of a cracking new album, *The Liberty Of Norton Folgate* at three sold-out Hackney Empire shows. Unusually, the record opens with a ten minute long title track, about Norton Folgate, a corner of East London, near Spitalfields, that was once legally independent from the rest of the capital. Not exactly standard nutty fare.

The album was released in May 2009 to critical praise (except in the *NME*) and popular acclaim, making the UK Top 5. They even appeared on a Catherine Tate Christmas special. What a fucking liberty! They even produced a new studio album in 2012.

And Lee Thompson formed a ska side-project called The Dance Brigade with Jennie Matthias AKA Jennie Bellestar.

Madness headlined a House Of Fun Weekender at Butlins, Minehead, in November 2011, three days of "fun and frolics" which seems neatly apt. This has become an annual event.

But perhaps the band's most impressive achievement was their appearance at the Queen's Golden Jubilee in June 2012, when they transformed Buck House into a terraced street courtesy of some amazing visuals. Millions of TV viewers watched in awe as the Nutty Boys took to the roof to perform classic hits accompanied by the creative light show. Suggs sang 'Our House' and 'It Must Be Love', as streets from around the country were projected onto the front of the palace. First came a row of terraced houses complete with a London bus and a black taxi cab going past it, then it changed to a town house and finally a large dolls house with kings and queens of yore also projected onto the Palace. Natch, Suggs changed the lyric in 'Our House' from 'in the middle of our street' to 'in the middle of one's street'.

As iconic moments go, it even topped the band's 2015 appearance on ITV's *Benidorm*. Madness have become a recognised component of English popular culture. Their success has surpassed all of their influences.

Away from the band, Suggsy has enjoyed the most solo success. He had hit albums and singles in the mid-Nineties and has appeared on TV, both as an actor and a documentary maker (these days generally on the History Channel.)

His first book, *Suggs & The City*, based on his *Disappearing London* TV series, was published in 2009. He brought out his autobiography, *Suggs: That Close*, in October 2013 and toured a successful one man show.

JUDGE DREAD

Judge Dread died on stage on March 13, 1998, just as he'd have wanted to go. He was 53.

His post 2-Tone singles such as 'Will I What' and 'My Name's Dick' failed to dent the charts, but were well received by aficionados of rude reggae. 'Will I What' in particular was a tour de filthy force, based around a disastrous chat-up encounter. The smooth-talking Judge invites his would-be darling to "Let's go round the topless bar/I know one that ain't too far", and asks "Would you let me feel your Bristols?/Would you let me take your drawers off" etc. It ends, unsurprisingly, with them exchanging insults: "Here, you seen one of these before?" "Yeah the last time I had a cocktail sausage!" "Bloody check, you wouldn't want it on the end of your nose for a wart." This is topped by the un-gentlemanly pay-off: "On yer bike and make sure the dog catcher don't see yer."

A couple of Dread's songs mentioned Snodland, the Medway town where he lived (the most memorable being 'The Belle Of Snodland Town': 'Virginia was her name/Virgin for short, but we all knew not for long...') and the town repaid the favour by naming a road Alex Hughes Close in his honour.

Alex died from a heart attack as he walked off stage at the end of a gig at Canterbury's Penny Theatre. His jovial writing partner Ted Lemon had passed away several years before, but Alex carried on writing and recording with ex-Bad Manners bass guitarist Nick Welsh. Later albums included 1989s *King Of Rudeness, Never Mind Up With The Cock, Here's Judge Dread* (1994), *Ska'd For Life*, and *Dread White and Blue*. The Harry May label celebrated his legacy by issuing *Judge Dread's Big Tin* containing his mightiest oeuvres. The Gonads, in our own small way, wrote and recorded a song called 'Badly Done' to honour his memory. It's utter filth.

BAD MANNERS

The hits dried up for Bad Manners after 1982s 'My Girl Lollipop' and they left Magnet Records the following year. Telstar released the TV-promoted compilation album, *The Height of Bad Manners*, which got them back in the album chart Top 30. The band signed with US label Portrait and they toured solidly for two years before deciding to call it a day in 1986.

But Buster couldn't let it lay. Within months he'd reformed the band with original members including Winston Bazoomies, Louis Alphonso,

Chris Kane and Martin Stewart. In 1988, Bad Manners licensed the Blue Beat Records label and set up an office in a barge in the back garden of Buster's house. Releases by themselves, *Napoleon Solo* and *Buster's Allstars* followed before the label folded in 1990.

This didn't stop them touring. In fact, nothing did. Nothing could.

In 1995, Buster moved to Margate in Kent, opening an outrageous seafront hotel which he called Fatty Towers and which he ran for three drunken, carb-heavy years.

In 1997, the band was signed by Moon Ska Records in the US who released the *Heavy Petting* album. In 2003, Buster started up another label of his own, Bad Records, releasing the album *Stupidity*. For two years, Manners headlined their own music festival known as Bad Fest (in 2005 and 2006) at RAF Twinwood Farm. This festival featured quality Ska, punk and Mod-related bands.

But any suggestion that Buster was toning down his act and going respectable was dramatically disproved when the fat man was banned from the Italian equivalent of *Top Of The Pops* for mooning on the show when the Pope was watching. ("How would I know the Pope was watching?" he asked indignantly).

Doug shot up to 32 stone, which was never going to be healthy. He collapsed on stage in Italy and subsequently required a gastric bypass. He says, "I lost some 15 stone. I lost so much weight people thought I was dying of AIDS or something and was about to die.

I was so used to carrying 30-odd stone that I found it easy to carry around less weight. When I got down to 12 stone I looked like a ballerina on stage. But I also looked quite gaunt and everyone was very worried about me. So you know what I turned to? That magical old drink called Guinness. And it podged me back up to 15 stone." Cheers!

The line-up changes constantly – Buster is now the only original member – but Bad Manners still play all over the world. In 2011, Buster recorded *Ska For Heroes* by Buster's Ska Battalion – basically a medley of songs from World War One ska-ed up - which is raising much-needed cash for forces-related charities. In true Buster style, he turned up at the recording studio with home-baked cherry pies for all, and his dog who barked along every time he sang.

Also in 2011, Cherry Red re-released the band's first four albums, *Ska' n' B, Loonee Tunes!, Gosh It's...Bad Manners*, and *Forging Ahead* on CD for the first time with bonus tracks. The albums were issued on their sister label, Pressure Drop.

Louis Alphonso Cook, known as the John Le Mesurier of Ska,

co-wrote all of the band's biggest hits including 'Lip Up Fatty', 'Special Brew', 'Lorraine', and 'Just a Feeling'. After leaving Bad Manners he joined Skaville UK with that great song-writer and bass-player Nick Welsh. Louis also played with Lee' Scratch' Perry, Judge Dread and Dave' Double Barrel' Barker.

Martin Stewart left Bad Manners in 1991, and performed with The Selecter on and off for 15 years. He later played in Skaville UK, who released two albums on the Moon Ska World label.

David Farren left in 1986; he was last seen playing in Stones tribute band The Rollin' Stoned, under the stage name of 'Keith Retched.'

Brian' Chew-It' Tuitt also quit for good in 1986; he runs his own rehearsal studios and lives in Kent. While Andrew Marson, another band member who left the same year, has worked as a carpenter in and around London. Paul Hyman lives in Enfield and has often guested with the Ska band, Too Many Crooks. Chris Kane is a session musician living in East London. He became a music teacher in the early Nineties and has performed live with The Jordanaires.

The last I heard Buster had moved off of his barge and had emigrated to Bulgaria where he is said to own "27 properties, and three of them even have roofs".

THE SELECTER

The wheels came off the Selecter soon after the gruelling US tour. Desmond Brown quit in the August 1980, and even Lynval Golding couldn't talk him into going back.

The band had split into two factions on the road, and this translated into a conflict of vision. Charley Anderson wanted the Selecter to get deeper and more heavily into reggae; Neol Davies wanted to head in a more experimental rock direction. Band management backed Neol, and soon Charley, who was suspected of fermenting dissent, had nowhere left to go but out of the door. Two days after Desmond quit, Pauline sacked him.

Charley and Desmond formed a band called The People which came to nothing, and then Chas joined H in the Century Steel Band. He also put together a Glasshouse Band package with Gaps to promote music on Coventry schools' curriculum, persuading the local council to cough up for £25,000 worth of gear. He dreamed of establishing a musical and arts centre but fell out with officials.

Charley moved to Sweden during the Nineties where he performed and recorded with The Skalatones; but now lives in South America. In

2009, he returned to Coventry to play a one-off concert at the Central Hall to promote his Ghetto Child charity project.

Charley 'H' Bembridge plays with Midlands-based the All Skas, and a UB40 tribute band called UB42.

After failing to get new group The Radio Beats noticed, Neol formed a new version of The Selecter with Pauline in 1991, but he left two years later to launch Selecter Instrumental, mostly playing movie tunes in a blue-beat style. In 1999, he released his 'Box of Blues' album on his own VoMatic label, assisted by Horace from the Specials and Anthony Harty. Another album, 'Future Swamp', followed featuring guests including Ronnie Wood.

Neol Davies made a return as The Selecter in January 2011 with a brand new ten-piece band, and an album featuring revamped versions of his classic hits.

Queen of Ska Pauline Black stayed in the spotlight longest. Re-signed solo by Chrysalis after Selecter break-up, she recorded a whole album with a gospel choir but fresh chart success eluded her. So in '82 she started concentrating on acting, winning awards for her portrayal of jazz singer Billie Holiday. Pauline acted on TV in Granada's *Something's Wrong In Paradise* (with August Darnell). She also presented a kids quiz show with Bob Carolgees, and turned her hand to serious TV journalism, presenting culture and politics show *Black On Black*.

She kept her hand in with musical projects such as the Supernatrals and Three Men & Black. But in October 2010, Pauline and charismatic co-singer Arthur "Gaps" Hendrickson played as The Selecter to celebrate the 30th anniversary of their seminal debut album, *Too Much Pressure*, performing the whole album live at the Sinners Day Festival in Belgium. In 2012, their new revitalised line-up toured the UK and Pauline published her 2-Tone memoir *Black By Design*. The band have been playing all over the world ever since, even appearing at Coachella and Glastonbury. They have released four new albums and the last tour saw them back in the UK Top 70. 2015s *Subculture* peaked at No 54.

Gwen Stefani cited Pauline as one of her formative influences and *Rolling Stone* magazine wrote 'Hands down, Pauline Black possessed the best voice that ever graced a 2-Tone release'.

THE BEAT

The Beat split in 1983. Dave Wakeling and Ranking Roger (Roger Charley) formed General Public and notched up a couple of decent hits in the USA, most notably with 'Tenderness'. General Public featured such luminaries as Mick Jones from The Clash, Mickey Billingham from Dexys, and Horace Panter from The Specials.

Other former Beat boys Andy Cox and David Steele formed the excellent Fine Young Cannibals with Roland Gift (previously singer with Ska band Akrylykz). Saxa and Everett Morton formed The International Beat along with singer Tony Beet. Ranking Roger produced their album, *The Hitting Line* (Blue Beat Records) in 1990. They split up two years later. Roger also joined the short-lived Big Audio Dynamite. Shortly after he joined the Special Beat hybrid. He has since recorded two solo albums. Roger's son Ranking Junior guested on The Ordinary Boys' hit single 'Boys Will Be Boys' and currently performs with UK line-up of The Beat, who released two new and well-received studio albums, 2016s *Bounce* and 2019s *Public Confidential*. In 2018 they released a live album and DVD called *The Beat – Live At The Roundhouse*.

Dave Wakeling fronts the US version of the group as The English Beat, who to confuse matters played the London International Ska Festival this year. Both the UK and US versions of the band toured regularly until this year. Sadly in March Roger died from cancer. He was 54.

KING HAMMOND

King Hammond was formed by Nick Welsh in 1987, back when he was playing bass in Bad Manners. His first King Hammond song was 'Skaville UK' which Buster nicked for a Bad Manners single. Two stand-alone King Hammond albums followed: *Revolution 70* and *Tank Tops & Hot Pants* (both later available as the double album, *Blow Your Mind*.)

In 1998, Nick reformed King Hammond to tour Europe with Laurel Aitken and Dave Barker. He formed Skaville UK, in 2006, releasing three critically acclaimed, glam-influenced studio albums. In 2010, he put King Hammond together again, and has since released three albums of high-quality original Ska songs such as *Cool Down Your Temper, Tattoo Girls, Riot In London Town* and *The Rudest Girl In Town* on his own N1 record label.

Nick has written with, played with and produced artists such as Prince Buster, Judge Dread, The Selecter, Selecter Acoustic, Buster's All-Stars, Dave Barker, Laurel Aitken, Judge Dread, and Rhoda Dakar. Other projects have included Big 5, a Ska-Punk hybrid with vocalist

Jennie Matthias (Belle Stars / Dance Brigade), and the all-star acoustic band 3 Men & Black, as well as co-writing the hit single 'This is Ska' with Longsy D.

Multi-talented Nick writes music for TV (*The Osbournes, Peep Show, Malcolm in the Middle*), computer games (*Smackdown versus Raw 2006, Day of Reckoning 2*) and the big screen (*Domino, The Magic Roundabout*). In 2002 Nick won a Grammy award for his work on the Lee' Scratch' Perry album Jamaican ET and was the MD on the live DVD, *The Ultimate Alien*. His own King Hammond 12-track album, *21st Century Scorchers* was released on vinyl last year.

The King has risen above his unfortunate affliction (Nick is a life-long West Bromwich Albion fan) and is generally considered to be a prince amongst men.

THE BODYSNATCHERS

The Bodysnatchers lasted for two singles before they folded, but singer Rhoda Dakar went on to enjoy a degree of success with The Special AKA, singing on her date rape song 'The Boiler' and 'Free Nelson Mandela.' In big demand as a session singer, she has worked with artists as varied as Apollo 440 and Dr Robert of the Blow Monkeys, but she has never forgotten her 2-Tone roots. She's guested with the Selecter, sung on the Madness album *The Liberty Of Norton Folgate* and appeared on the 3 Men & Black tour with Dave Wakeling, Roddy Radiation, Nick Welsh and Pauline Black. Rhoda co-wrote her solo album *Cleaning In Another Woman's Kitchen* with Nick Welsh. It was released by Moon Ska World in 2007 to much critical acclaim.

In 2015 she released the album *Rhoda Dakar Sings The Bodysnatchers* and has since released *The Lotek Four volumes one and two*. Rhoda also DJed on the Selecter's last US tour.

After the Bodysnatchers split, the bulk of the band – Stella, SJ, Miranda, Penny and Judy – formed a new combo called The Bellestars bringing in the wonderfully bubbly Jennie Mathias as lead singer and Lesley Stone on bass. They were rapidly signed by Stiff and supported The Beat and Madness.

Their first three singles flopped but finally broke their duck with a cover of 'Iko Iko' which went Top 40 in 1982, followed by more covers – 'The Clapping Song' made the Top 20.

In January 1983 they released their biggest hit, 'Sign of the Times', which made the Top 3 and charted all over Europe. They never repeated the success. But they ploughed on, shedding members regularly, until they finally called it a day.

And then 'Iko Iko' became a US Top 20 smash in 1989. D'oh!

Jennie Matthias continued to perform. She guested on two Skaville UK albums, and the Gonads track 'Long Ska Summer'. In 2010, she formed new ska band Dance Brigade with Lee Thompson from Madness, and started to perform in her new band 1-Stop-Experience before turning her back on the music business to work in a charity shop.

THE BEAT GOES ON

Ska continues to be a hit with music lovers all over the world, spawning fusions like Ska Punk, and the harder Ska-core; Jazz Ska and even Oi-Tone. This is not the right place to run through the many great US Ska and Ska-punk bands who brightened up the Nineties – they deserve a book of their own. But if you're interested, here's a quick look at the most interesting Ska bands around today: The Smooth Beans (Spain), The Aggrolites (LA), The Bullets (LA), The Carolregians (Belgium), Green Room Rockers (Mid West, USA), Magic Touch (Germany), The Ratazanas (Portugal), The Upsessions (Holland).

Since I wrote that in the first edition, Ska bands have continue to emerge all over the globe, especially in Mexico and California. The Interrupters formed in 2011 and look like the band most likely to make it globally. They signed to Hellcat/Epitaph and have released three albums – *The Interrupters, Say It Out Loud* and *Fight The Good Fight*. To these ears, they have taken 2-Tone and recreated it in their own image. Songs like 'Take Back The Power' and 'She's Kerosene' are better than anything I've heard for a long time.

The Aggrolites released their album *Reggae Now* this year and established themselves as purveyors of a 1969 Tighten Up style sound.

At home, the Dualers from south east London continue to impress live and I've got a real soft spot for Buster Shuffle who call themselves "Ska punk rock and roll" and have been supporting Less Than Jake.

Sadly nothing became of the Dub City Rockers, although their song 'Trojan City Love' says it all. Ska may not sell as many records as it once did, but it's as sure as hell not going away!

CLUB SKA

London's Club Ska is the great Ska success story of the Noughties. It's widely regarded as the premier club of its kind in the UK – yet it all began eleven years ago with a series of coincidences, when Mark Wyeth (who's played bass for Laurel Aitken, Foxy's Ruts and Symarip) broke down on a roundabout in Ickenham. The driver who stopped to help turned out to be promoter Dave Beal who was putting Dr Feelgood on that night at The Rayners venue in Rayners Lane in near-by Harrow. Mark went along and met Nick the landlord, a man so keen on Bad Manners that he called his two dogs' Buster' and 'Brew'. Learning that Mark knew Buster, Nick asked if he could get Bad Manners to play there. But the Rayners was known as a rock/blues venue (with jazz bands on Sunday dinnertimes), so Mark and Dave suggested a Bad Manners show would only made sense in the context of a regular Ska night. They were knocking on an open door.

Club Ska 2000 was born – the 'Club Ska' taken from the Sixties albums of that name – and Bad Manners played the opening. A year later they dropped the '2000' and registered 'Club Ska' as a trademark. Their idea was simple – to present the best authentic bluebeat and original reggae in a friendly setting.

Mark, now a QC, had loved Ska since catching the original 2-ToneTour at Leicester's De Montfort Hall in October 1979. He explains: "Our shows were to be more than just a gig; a Club Ska show would feature two great live groups/performers along with an MC and live DJs playing the best Ska and reggae vinyl on our own sound system. We placed a heavy emphasis and focus on dancing and in particular 'dancing the Ska'. "(Later, they worked with Dr Dodds, Surrey University's Head of Dance Studies, and helped with her research into the origins of 'skanking'.)

"Our watchword was respect," says Mark. "There was a large body of great Jamaican music to which little or no attention was being given. Great artists like Laurel Aitken and Derrick Morgan performed mostly in Europe – not in the UK. With the exception of Gaz's Rocking Blues in the West End there were no regular live Ska shows in the London area at the time."

Club Ska has two rules: 1) EVERYBODY HAS FUN. 2) NO POLITICS. Their message was simply and memorably delivered by Laurel Aitken from their stage: "We love you – we simply, simply love you. So hit it from the top to the very last drop".

Laurel gave his last ever stage performance at Club Ska in 2005 (see the DVD 'Laurel Aitken and friends – Live at Club Ska'.) Live albums with The Riffs and Symarip have also been recorded and released at Club Ska.

In 2010 the club moved sticks to the 100 Club on Oxford Street and had a grand opening night with 'Skinhead Moonstomp' legends Symarip featuring the vocal talent of original lead singer Roy Ellis – one of the forefathers of 2Tone movement and inventor of Skinhead Reggae.

As I write Roy and his Moonstompers perform at Club Ska on Saturday July 6, 2019. There's no stopping this thing.

RIP CARDBOARD

Sadly Steve Eaton passed away in March 2011, aged 51. Known as 'Cardboard', Coventry rude boy Steve was the Specials' first roadie – and much more. He was pretty much tour managing them after the Bernie Rhodes debacle. Cardboard was regarded as a style icon by all on the Coventry scene. He looked so cool, the Selecter's Neol Davies asked him to pose for their *Too Much Pressure* album cover. When the 2-Tone Wall Of Fame was launched in Coventry Steve Eaton was one of the first six names added to it. He was a Ska DJ at the beginning, and had been a publican in London with wife Lindsey; but music was always his first love. Steve became a punk promoter in Coventry, and was heavily into German industrial sounds. He had suffered with throat cancer for three years and heart trouble, which killed him. Lindsey says "Towards the end he started to teach me to DJ, it was almost as if he knew he didn't have long to go."

Lindsey Eaton DJed at the Specials pre-gig party in Coventry in October 2011, and carried on as Lady Cardboard in Steve's honour.

RIP PRINCE BUSTER

Prince Buster, the Jamaican Ska legend who gave the world 'Madness' and 'One Step Beyond' sadly died in September 2016 aged 78.

Born in Orange Street, Kingston, railway worker's son Cecil Bustamente Campbell earned his nickname in the boxing ring – he was trained by Sid Brown, the middleweight champion of Jamaica – but became a champ in another field, the music business first as a producer and then a performer.

And Clement "Coxsone" Dodd can take some of the credit. Impressed by Buster's quick wit and confidence, Dodd took him on as a security man and PA.

In the late Fifties, Buster moved on to set up a record store, and then his own sound system, the Voice of the People before entering the recording studio. One of his earliest productions was the Folkes Brothers' hit 'Oh Carolina'. Buster is said to have asked the guitarist Jah Jerry to emphasise the after beat rather than the downbeat. Ska was born.

Prince Buster had his first British hit in 1965 with 'Al Capone', the song resurrected by the Specials on their debut single 'Gangsters'. (TV talking heads often claim Bob Marley was the first reggae star to reach Britain, Buster did it ten years before – he was on Ready Steady Go in 1964, as was Millie Small).

As the song says 'Buster he sold the heat, with a rocksteady beat…'

Judge Dread, the former bouncer and wrestler Alex Hughes, acquired his stage name from Prince Buster's song of that name, as did Madness (who were originally called Morris & The Minors).

Buster's influence waned in the seventies – he'd converted to Islam and wasn't comfortable with the Rasta tide – but when the nutty boys eulogised him on their debut 45, 'The Prince' and recorded his 'One Step Beyond' a fresh generation learned about his genius.

If there's a message from Prince Buster's passing it can be found in another of his splendid songs: 'Enjoy yourself, it's later than you think…'

Prince Buster, born 26 May 1938, died 8th September 2016

RIP RICO

Rico Rodriguez died four years ago. The veteran Ska trombonist is probably best remembered for playing on The Specials' chart-topping Ghost Town and their version of Dandy Livingstone's A Message to You, Rudy (he played on the original too). Cuban born Emmanuel Rodriguez was part of the Jamaican Ska scene from the start, but came to England in the early sixties where he performed with Georgie Fame and his Blue Flames. Rico worked with everyone from Prince Buster to Jools Holland via Laurel Aitken and Sting, and gets a mention from Ian Dury in Reasons To Be Cheerful. I was lucky enough to meet him more than thirty years ago, and saw him perform with the Specials in New York. He was a wise, humble man with a love of the reggae musician's traditional relaxant of choice. On that US tour, the band played Canada. Coming back into the US Rico carefully concealed his weed in his bible only to get pulled up by US Customs for transporting oranges – which he'd actually bought in the US days before. I saw him again a few years ago and had been due to honour him at the Heritage Of Ska event a week after he died. His solo album *Man From Wareika* still stands the test of time. Died September 4 , 2015.

DANCE CRAZE

01-261 6153

THE SKA REVIVAL

01-261 6153

NUTTY BOYS + GIRLS

355 CHARTWELL SQUARE VICTORIA CIRCUS, SOUTHEND-ON-SEA Tel: 610432

MECCA of course! **[Zhivago's]** presents

A FANTASTIC NIGHT OUT WITH

THE LEEPERS ★ NUMBER 6

plus *DISCO*

TUESDAY, 29th APRIL 1980

This special ticket will admit one person
for only £1 (normal admission charge £1.50) before 10.30 pm

The management reserve the right to refuse admission

DOORS OPEN 8 pm   OVER 18's ONLY

DANISH
MADNESS
SKINS

CANVEY BOB

Odeon Theatre
LEWISHAM B.F.13

ODEON THEATRE
LEWISHAM B.F.13

STRAIGHT MUSIC PRESENTS

MADNESS

Circle   CIRCLE

O18   **O18**

BLOCK G

TO BE GIVEN UP   NO TICKET EXCHANGED NOR MONEY REFUNDED
                      THIS PORTION TO BE RETAINED   [P.T.O.]

CAMDEN BOYS

DANCE CRAZE

SUNBURY SKINS

CATFORD CHRIS

SKINS FROM BOGNOR

DANNY DC

ABOUT THE AUTHOR

GARRY BUSHELL was born and raised in South East London. He started his career on the rock weekly Sounds, interviewing everyone from The Clash and Steel Pulse to Blondie, U2, the Specials and Iron Maiden. The son of a fireman and a bank secretary, he is best known for his award winning Bushell On The Box TV column. Garry managed punk bands the Cockney Rejects, The Blood and Maninblack; his own group the Gonads have been going for 42years without any noticeable success, and his Rancid Sounds punk and Ska show appears regularly on 2nd City Radio. He has five children and four grandchildren, and lives in Kent.

ACKNOWLEDGEMENTS

SPECIAL (AKA) THANKS TO.
Neville and Christine Staple, Pauline Black, Douglas Trendle, Cathal Smyth, Paul Pettitt, Mark Wyeth, Brian Ska Morgan, Paul Williams, Pete Chambers, King Hammond, Rhoda Dakar and Paul Hallam (The Stalin of Style).

MORE SPECIAL THANKS TO.
Sharon Brennan, Nicky Porter, Karena Marcum, Graham Buckland, Jake Bonnici (and his Dad), Riaz Khan, Gary Loveridge and Moira Rhodes, The staff of the Royal Exchange, Vino our fave Albanian, Paul Cookie Cook, Jeff the Fish, Tom McCourt, Tim Wells, Cass P, Ennio & the Turin Boys, Ed Piller and all at Acid Jazz, Dei Treanor for all things editorial first time around, Roger Allen, Tony Meary, Mr DDC, Alan Handscombe and the Camden Stylists, Symon Jones, Bryan Conyers, Ronnie the Mod Plumber, Barry Mingard, Chris and Joeli Dale, Gordon Rutter - Nigel Mitchell and the Sunbury Skins, Jean Pierre Boutellier, Wayne Darby, Clelia Lucchitta, Soren/Morten & Martin from Denmark, Toni Fox, Paul Emuss, Mik Whitnall and the 100 Men, Sharon Tyler, Anne Griffin, Darrel Ball, James Travis, Larissa Collins, Emilie West, Dave Edwards and Andrea, Tricia Redding, The Dualers, Bob Piper from Our Price records, Maddy and Bob, John Whitwell, Mr Bingley - Present and Lilith, Callum and Jodie, Lucas and Katie, Allie Mayor, Gary Evans, Karl Overhand, Andy Rider and Susan Jones, Nick Welsh, Ani H for writing scrapbook words, Ollie and Izzy Roche, Andy Fawcett, Ed Silvester, Andy Clarke CV1, Petr Ruzika, James Travis, Pauline Swindon (Work), Julia Fallon, Simone and Stev, Beth and Mark Huxley, Steve the Fleece, Lucia Hall, Tony Rackley, Mark Spinks and Tom Varey, David Price, John Marrable, Mr Bingley, Lilith and Preston (Do the Dog - not the Donkey) and Mrs H for putting up with bits of paper all over the dining room table again again. Plus the 100s of people we have forgotten I'm sure (we will remember third edition honest).

In memory of Barney Dowling 7th May 1959-15th December 2018

A rude boy bedroom from the ska revival era as recreated at The Coventry Music Museum. It is located at the 2-Tone Village, The Courtyard, 74-80 Walsgrave Road, CV2 4ED. Check the web site to find when the museum, Wall of Fame, café and 2-Tone shop are open www.covmm.co.uk

PHOTOGRAPHERS

David Arnoff   Toni Tye   Virginia Turbett

DAVID ARNOFF

Many photographs in this book were taken by David Arnoff in the Summer/Autumn of 1980 in Los Angeles. He was born in Cleveland, Ohio – as was rock 'n' roll itself as he's keen to point out. His family moved to California in the Sixties, a prime time and location for all things musical & countercultural. He started photographing at the onset of punk, an early highlight being the cover of the Cramps debut album. David moved to London in 1984 and hasn't looked back since, preferring to be a citizen of a country that, among other things, understands 2-Tone. Find more of his photos at davidarnoff.com

TONI TYE

Back in 1980 while living in the Midlands Toni was invited to shoot stills (for a proposed book on 2 Tone). These shoots were the rehearsals and gigs that became the film *Dance Craze*. The shoots focused on the scene, The Kids, the Skinheads, The Fashions and some of the bands backstage. Many of these unique photos are featured in this book. Find more at tonitye.com

VIRGINIA TURBETT

She was a teenage punk who became one of Sounds' best-loved photographers. I first met her on a Right To Work march in 1978. She was a fan of the revolutionary socialist punk band Crisis, whose female following were known as 'the Effects of Crisis'.

She took great pictures so I encouraged her to become a pro. Virg accompanied me on many an adventure, including The Jam in Sheffield, Secret Affair in Southend and perhaps more glamorously the Modettes in Los Angeles.

She was professional, principled and fun to be around. Bands took to her easily and her pictures - some of which are included in this book - were always terrific. Virginia has lots more pictures where these came from and they can be purchased by contacting her on virginia@virginiaturbett.com

---

OTHER TITLES BY GARRY BUSHELL

'79 Ska Revival: Dance Craze
Sounds Of Glory Volumes 1 & 2
Cockney Reject (with Jeff Turner)
Running Free
Hoolies
The Face
Two-Faced
Face Down
All Or Nothing
Hell Bent
Bushell On The Rampage
1,001 Reasons Why EastEnders Is Pony
I Had A Good Eight Inches Last Night
The World According To Garry Bushell

SECRET AFFAIR

THE CHORDS

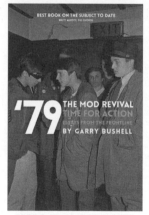

MODS AT BRIDGE HOUSE

PURPLE HEARTS

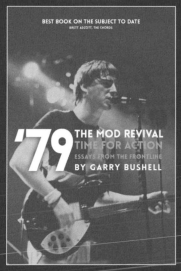

MADNESS

THE BEAT

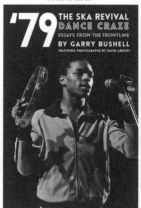

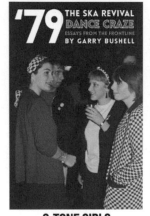

2-TONE GIRLS

THE SELECTER

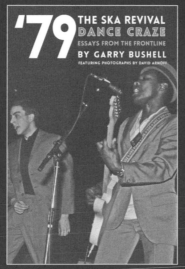